La La Land

OXFORD GUIDES TO FILM MUSICALS

Dominic Broomfield-McHugh, Series Editor

Love Me Tonight
Geoffrey Block

Singin' in the Rain
Andrew Buchman

La La Land
Hannah Lewis

La La Land

HANNAH LEWIS

OXFORD
UNIVERSITY PRESS

Oxford University Press is a department of the University of Oxford.
It furthers the University's objective of excellence in research, scholarship,
and education by publishing worldwide. Oxford is a registered trademark of
Oxford University Press in the UK and in certain other countries.

Published in the United States of America by Oxford University Press
198 Madison Avenue, New York, NY 10016, United States of America.

© Oxford University Press 2024

Library of Congress Cataloging-in-Publication Data
Names: Lewis, Hannah, 1985– author.
Title: La La Land / Hannah Lewis.
Description: New York : Oxford University Press, 2024. |
Series: Oxford guides to film musicals | Includes bibliographical references and index.
Identifiers: LCCN 2024020053 (print) | LCCN 2024020054 (ebook) |
ISBN 9780197791950 (paperback) | ISBN 9780197682586 (hardback) |
ISBN 9780197682593 (epub) | ISBN 9780197682616
Subjects: LCSH: La La Land (Motion picture : 2016)
Classification: LCC PN1997.2.L35 L49 2024 (print) | LCC PN1997.2.L35 (ebook) |
DDC 791.43/72—dcundefined
LC record available at https://lccn.loc.gov/2024020053
LC ebook record available at https://lccn.loc.gov/2024020054

DOI: 10.1093/9780197682616.001.0001

The manufacturer's authorised representative in the EU for product safety is
Oxford University Press España S.A. of El Parque Empresarial San Fernando
de Henares, Avenida de Castilla, 2 – 28830 Madrid (www.oup.es/en or
product.safety@oup.com). OUP España S.A. also acts as importer into Spain
of products made by the manufacturer.

Contents

List of Figures   vii
List of Musical Examples   ix
Series Editor's Foreword   xi
Acknowledgments   xiii

Introduction   1

1. The Development of a "Realist Musical": The Chazelle–Hurwitz
   Collaboration   9

2. Nostalgia, Homage, and Bittersweet Endings:
   La La Land and the Classic Film Musical   30

3. Modernizing a Classic Form: Realism and Virtuosic
   Performance   61

4. *La La Land* and Jazz   79

5. Reception   99

Conclusion: *La La Land*'s Legacy   113

Notes   117
Bibliography   125
Index   135

Figures

1.1a–b	"Love in the Fall," *Guy and Madeline on a Park Bench* (2009)	17
2.1a–b	Opening, *Les Demoiselles de Rochefort* (1967), and "Another Day of Sun," *La La Land* (2016)	46
2.2a–b	"There's Got to Be Something Better Than This," *Sweet Charity* (1969), and "Someone in the Crowd," *La La Land* (2016)	50
2.3a–c	"Isn't It a Lovely Day," *Top Hat* (1935), "Dancing in the Dark," *The Band Wagon* (1953), and "A Lovely Night," *La La Land* (2016)	53
3.1 a–f	"Another Day of Sun," *La La Land*	72
3.2	Planetarium Scene, *La La Land*	73
3.3	"Audition," *La La Land*	74
4.1a–b	"Herman's Habit," *La La Land*	85
4.2a–b	"Summer Montage/Madeline," *La La Land*	86
4.3a–f	"Start a Fire," *La La Land*	94
5.1	Saturday Night Live *La La Land* Interrogation Sketch, January 2017	100
5.2	*La La Land* producer Jordan Horowitz holds up the Best Picture envelope at the 2017 Academy Awards	110

Musical Examples

1.1	"Love in the Fall" (excerpt), *Guy and Madeline on a Park Bench* (2009) (my transcription)	16
1.2a–b	"A Lovely Night" (excerpts), Gosling's vocal parts, *La La Land* (2016)	25
2.1a	Michel Legrand, "Chanson des Jumelles" (excerpt), *Les Demoiselles de Rochefort* (1967) (my transcription)	44
2.1b	Justin Hurwitz, "A Lovely Night" (excerpt), *La La Land* (2016)	44
2.2	"City of Stars" (excerpt), *La La Land* (2016)	55
4.1	"Summer Montage/Madeline," excerpt (my transcription), *La La Land* (2016)	86
4.2	Mia & Sebastian's Theme (excerpt), *La La Land* (2016)	98

Series Editor's Foreword

Hailed upon its release as "a fizzy fantasy and a hard-headed fable"[1] by the *New York Times*, *La La Land* (2016) quickly became a favorite with audiences and admired amongst critics. Yet a gaffe at the Academy Awards ceremony, whereby *La La Land* was erroneously announced as the winner of the award for Best Picture, had a dramatic impact on the film's reception that led to a wider discourse on aspects of representation in the movie.

This lively volume from Hannah Lewis offers a thoughtful study of both content and context, examining the film's origins and assessing what it has come to mean during the cultural shifts we have seen in the years since its release. Benefiting from interviews with director Damien Chazelle, songwriters Justin Hurwitz, Benj Pasek, and Justin Paul, and choreographer Mandy Moore, Lewis's book provides equal insights into what the filmmakers were trying to achieve and how audiences have reacted to it.

The opening chapter considers the relationship between Chazelle and Hurwitz, college roommates at Harvard who went on to make several films together, including the acclaimed *Whiplash* (2014). Lewis reveals that a common theme of their movies—which also include the more recent, controversial *Babylon* (2022)—is the price paid by ambitious people for striving for the difficult. The complicated road to success with *La La Land* is uncovered thanks to Lewis's interviews with the creators and the chapter shows how Chazelle and Hurwitz's "artistic journey is a case of life imitating art."

Nostalgia forms the focus of the second chapter, with Lewis demonstrating how *La La Land* is "packed" with "intertextual references to classic film musicals in its music, narrative, sets, costumes, and cinematography," including a nod to the title number of *Singin' in the Rain* (1952), another movie covered in the *Guides to Film Musicals* series. Lewis lays out how *La La Land* manages to have its cake and eat it too: the film invokes the warm feelings associated with classic movie musicals but also reframes many of them, resulting in a critical gesture about the nature of nostalgia itself.

That reality check forms the focus of the third chapter, which deals with how Chazelle ultimately made *La La Land* into a realistic film, despite the reliance on "the stylized audiovisual and narrative codes of classic Hollywood."

This gives way to a special focus on jazz in the fourth chapter: an important topic for both director and composer, and one they have addressed in several films. Lewis's nuanced discussion of positionality provides a welcome critique of the movie here: She notes that "the jazz narrative is the aspect where *La La Land*'s centering of white perspectives and experience, and therefore its broader racial problematic, becomes most clearly apparent."

The book concludes with a discussion of the reception of *La La Land*, looking at the strength of feeling it has evoked in people, whether positive or negative. "[By] bringing many ongoing debates about the film musical into the contemporary age," writes Lewis, "it has shown how the genre is uniquely situated to function as a lightning rod for broader cultural conversations." In turn, Lewis's book provides rich insights into how evoking popular culture of the past has implications for who we are today—a reminder of the pleasure and pain of loving musicals.

Dominic Broomfield-McHugh
Series Editor
Oxford Guides to Film Musicals

Acknowledgments

I am grateful to the many individuals who made this book possible. First and foremost, I would like to thank the artists behind *La La Land* who so generously agreed to speak with me over Zoom or on the phone during the first summer of the pandemic: Damien Chazelle, Justin Hurwitz, Mandy Moore, Benj Pasek, and Justin Paul. Thank you for sharing your perspectives on the creative process and your experiences in making this film, which has made my account of *La La Land* much more nuanced and engaging. I am grateful to Dom Broomfield-McHugh for inviting me to contribute this book to the series, and for his kind, thoughtful, and insightful feedback as Series Editor; and to Norman Hirschy at Oxford University Press, for his encouragement and guidance every step of the way. The research and writing of this book were made possible through the financial support of a Butler Faculty Development Award from the University of Texas at Austin Butler School of Music.

The book additionally benefited immensely from the ideas, expertise, and kindness of other friends and colleagues who provided various kinds of support along the way. Elizabeth Craft, Louis Epstein, Frank Lehman, and Matt Mugmon provided invaluable feedback on my manuscript at various stages in the writing process. Thanks to Erin Maher for her keen editorial eye when copyediting my text. Jim Buhler has helped me and my work in countless ways. And a special thanks to Carol Oja for sparking my renewed interest in musicals in graduate school, which prompted me to take them seriously as subjects of my research and teaching.

And last, but certainly not least, I am forever grateful for the love and support of my family. To my parents, Jan and Dan, and my sister Becca, thanks for encouraging my creative and scholarly endeavors from the beginning. To my husband, Ojas, thank you for the constant intellectual and emotional support. And to my two children, Anjali and Rohan, I love you more than I can say, and I hope you are inspired to find and pursue your passions and dreams, whatever they may be.

Introduction

"And the Academy Award for Best Picture [goes to . . .] *La La Land!*" When presenters Warren Beatty and Faye Dunaway announced the 2017 Best Picture winner, the film musical's Oscars triumph seemed inevitable, even pre-ordained. The film had already won numerous awards that night, after receiving enthusiastic critical praise and warm audience reception since its summer 2016 premiere at film festivals. *La La Land* was a love letter to Hollywood, heralded as the film that would reinvigorate the Hollywood musical genre; the Best Picture win was merely a sign that Hollywood loved *La La Land* back. But as the producers began their acceptance speeches that night, it became clear that something was wrong. Beatty and Dunaway had been given the wrong card, mistakenly announcing the wrong film. In fact, *Moonlight,* a small-budget film about the coming of age of a queer Black man, had won the Oscar for Best Picture.

This awkward mix-up was in many ways symbolic of *La La Land*'s broader cultural reception since its premiere. The first popular Hollywood musical of the twenty-first century with an original screenplay, it was welcomed with ease into the contemporary canon of great films by critics and audiences alike, as journalists praised the film for "mak[ing] musicals matter again."[1] Directed by Damien Chazelle with music by Justin Hurwitz, two relative newcomers to Hollywood, the film told the story of a romance between aspiring actress Mia and jazz pianist Sebastian as the two pursued their dreams in Los Angeles. It contemporized the classic Hollywood musical, using a vintage form to tell a modern story: While paying nostalgic homage to such classics as *Singin' in the Rain, West Side Story, The Umbrellas of Cherbourg,* and the Astaire-Rogers films of the 1930s, it depicted a modern romance with realist, contemporary sensibilities. This blend of nostalgia and realism made it an instant classic, and it won a record-breaking seven Golden Globes and a record-tying fourteen Oscar nominations. At the same time, the way *La La Land* unwittingly stole *Moonlight*'s thunder at the Oscars encapsulated some critiques of the film that had emerged in the intervening months since its premiere, particularly regarding the story's treatment of race. Though its

La La Land. Hannah Lewis, Oxford University Press. © Oxford University Press 2024.
DOI: 10.1093/9780197682616.003.0001

nostalgic approach to the film musical was celebrated by some, others began to suggest that this nostalgia was problematic, especially at a cultural moment when Hollywood was beginning to grapple more fully with its fraught history of representation onscreen. The Oscars mix-up symbolized the messiness of Hollywood's reckoning with its own past, and within that story, *La La Land* emerges as a film that looked backward in some ways and forward in others. Indeed, in both its praise and its critiques, *La La Land* and its reception reveal much about the film musical genre's enduring and evolving place in contemporary American culture, and about America itself.

As a scholar and fan of the film musical genre, I was excited by the critical attention *La La Land* received when it first came out, and I was eager to see it myself. I saw it in a packed movie theater in late December 2016 in Austin, Texas. The energetic opening number, "Another Day of Sun," immediately drew me in through its stunning visuals and its blend of old and new. But as the film continued, I had a range of reactions, and by the end, I found myself feeling deeply ambivalent about what I had just seen. Some aspects of *La La Land* really spoke to me: the leading couple felt incredibly real, and modern, as they struggled to navigate their career ambitions and maintain their relationship. I was also taken by many of the references to earlier film musicals that I love, and I enjoyed the moments of recognition when I would catch a reference. At the same time, I found myself disappointed by other aspects. I was frustrated by the film's racial representation—particularly its whiteness and its portrayal of jazz—and worried about the kind of message it sent about race in contemporary American society. From an aesthetic standpoint, I wanted more from the musical numbers: I wanted the rest of the songs and dances to transport me just as the opening scene had, but I just could not get over the lack of musical and choreographic training of the otherwise quite talented leading couple. It is precisely my ambivalence about the film that has kept me returning to it since the first time I saw it. *La La Land* offers me an opportunity to clarify for myself just what I find so magical about the film musical genre that *La La Land* pays homage to, and what it means for viewers (myself included) when these elements are transposed to the 21st century.

La La Land is a love story, but it is also about pursuing one's dreams, and reckoning with the personal cost that comes with those pursuits. (See Table 0.1 for a list of the film's musical numbers.) The film's opening number highlights this theme: during a traffic jam on the freeway that transforms into a spontaneous, joyful song and dance ("Another Day of Sun"), members of the ensemble sing about the various challenges and setbacks of trying to pursue their dreams in L.A. After this opening number, we are introduced to the leading couple: Mia Dolan, an aspiring actress, and Sebastian "Seb" Wilder, a jazz pianist, both getting nowhere in their careers. Mia works at a coffee shop at the Warner Bros. backlot while attending countless unsuccessful auditions, and Seb is struggling to pay the bills but unwilling to compromise on the style of music he wants to play. Their challenges are articulated through musical numbers—Mia's in "Someone in the Crowd," where she attends a demoralizing Hollywood Hills party with her roommates, and Seb's in the instrumental number "Mia & Sebastian's Theme," where he strays from the setlist at his restaurant gig to play his own music and is fired as a result. Mia happens to walk by and hears Seb play, but he brushes her off as he storms out of the restaurant.

Months later, the two encounter each other at a party where Seb is playing synthesizer in a 1980s pop cover band. As they leave the party and walk to their cars, they comment on the "waste of a lovely night" together while dancing in front of a beautiful sunset ("A Lovely Night"). Seb visits Mia at her workplace, and the two finally connect. They stroll around the Warner Bros. backlot and discuss their passions and dreams. When Mia claims to "hate jazz," Seb takes her to a jazz club and expresses his desire to open his own club ("Herman's Habit"). After they part ways, Seb sings to himself on the pier, wondering if this is the start of a romance or another dream that will not be fulfilled ("City of Stars"). The two meet up for a screening of *Rebel Without a Cause*, then visit the Griffith Observatory, where they dance together and embrace ("Planetarium").

Seb and Mia begin a whirlwind romance ("Summer Montage/ Madeline"). As their romance deepens, they start to confront their personal disappointments and frustrations in their respective careers. After another unsuccessful audition, Mia, at the encouragement of Seb, quits her job to write and perform a one-woman play. Seb, who has been playing a regular but low-paying gig at a jazz club, encounters his former bandmate Keith, who invites him to be keyboardist in a fusion band called the Messengers. Seb reluctantly accepts, feeling he is selling out but hoping to prove to Mia and himself that he can find success as a musician. Although Mia and Seb are very much in love, their relationship begins to strain as they pursue different aspects of their careers ("City of Stars" Reprise). Mia attends one of the Messengers' concerts, and despite the band's popularity, she can tell it is not the style of music Seb wants to play ("Start a Fire"). In the meantime, because

Table 0.1 Musical Numbers in *La La Land*

Song/Number Title	Time Stamp	Characters Performing	Description
"Another Day of Sun"	0:00:59–0:04:43	Ensemble (singing and dancing)	Upbeat tempo; full orchestration; built on syncopated rhythmic gesture in the accompaniment; full ensemble choreography; appears to be filmed in a single continuous shot
"Someone in the Crowd"	0:10:40–0:15:17	Mia and her roommates; ensemble (singing and dancing)	Upbeat tempo; full orchestration; begins in apartment, moves to outside the apartment, then montage of L.A. and Mia at the party; solo piano accompanies Mia's solo section; slow-motion ensemble choreography as the tempo increases and orchestration builds back up for the final ensemble chorus
"Mia & Sebastian's Theme"	0:16:16–0:17:31;0:23:09–0:24:48	Sebastian (solo piano)	Slow rubato waltz with a jazz improvised flourish at the end; played twice, the first time from Mia's perspective as she passes the restaurant, and the second time from Sebastian's perspective as he plays inside the restaurant
"A Lovely Night"	0:32:16–0:36:11	Mia and Sebastian (singing and dancing)	Relaxed swinging tempo, harmonically structured around circle of fifths; Sebastian sings one verse, then Mia responds with a verse of her own, followed by an extended dance; song interrupted by Mia's cell phone ringing
"Herman's Habit"	0:43:06–0:44:50	Jazz combo (instrumental)	Hard bop instrumental number played by a diegetic quintet (tenor sax, trumpet, and rhythm section); Sebastian and Mia sit watching the musicians and talking to each other as the band plays
"City of Stars"	0:46:15–0:48:00	Sebastian (singing)	Slow minor-key ballad, sparse orchestration; begins with a single piano line; Sebastian whistles the piano's melody before and after singing

Table 0.1 Continued

Song/Number Title	Time Stamp	Characters Performing	Description
"Planetarium"	0:54:32–0:58:47	Mia and Sebastian (dancing)	Begins as musical underscoring; orchestral arrangement of "Mia & Sebastian's Theme" slowly building in intensity and volume as the couple floats in the air and dances in the stars
"Summer Montage/ Madeline"	0:59:48–1:01:50	Mia and Sebastian (dancing); Sebastian and jazz combo (playing)	Hard bop instrumental number played by Sebastian's ensemble; begins as instrumental, underscoring Mia and Sebastian's blossoming romance; becomes diegetic as Mia dances while Sebastian plays at the Lighthouse Café
"City of Stars" (reprise)	1:08:21–1:12:58	Mia and Sebastian (singing)	Begins with Sebastian playing piano and singing, then Mia joins in; music continues (full orchestra) over a montage of the couple taking steps in their respective careers that will end up straining their relationship; ends with a return to them singing at the piano
"Start a Fire"	1:13:03–1:16:02	The Messengers (sung by Keith and backup singers)	Jazz-inflected pop music, played by the band onstage; begins with a piano solo by Sebastian and becomes progressively cheesier and more over-the-top
"Audition (The Fools Who Dream)"	1:37:43–1:41:03	Mia (singing)	Slow $\frac{3}{4}$; begins a cappella, piano enters, then orchestra builds up; Mia sings standing in place as the camera slowly zooms in, then arcs around her
"Epilogue"	1:50:18–1:58:15	Mia, Sebastian, and ensemble (dancing)	Begins with Sebastian playing "Mia & Sebastian's Theme" on the piano; transitions into a dream ballet depicting an alternate ending to Mia and Sebastian's romance where they end up together; instrumental medley of the songs from the film

of his commitments with the band, he misses Mia's play. Mia, disheartened by her play's poor attendance, decides to abandon her acting ambitions and moves back home to Boulder City, Nevada.

Seb then receives a call from a casting director who attended Mia's play and is trying to reach her to invite her to audition for a film. He drives to Boulder City to persuade her to return to Los Angeles for the audition. At the audition, the casting director asks her to tell a story, and she sings about her aunt, who had inspired her to pursue her dreams ("Audition [The Fools Who Dream]"). Afterward, Mia and Seb contemplate the future of their careers and decide that they must each pursue their respective dreams, even if it means their paths will diverge.

Five years later, Mia is a famous actress, married to a different man. One night on a date, they happen upon a small basement jazz club. They go in, and Mia discovers that Seb is the owner. He notices her in the crowd while performing onstage and begins to play their love theme. His music prompts a dream sequence where the two imagine what might have been had they stayed in their relationship ("Epilogue"). The two share a silent, meaningful glance before returning to reality. The film thus ends on a bittersweet note: Mia and Seb have achieved their dreams, but at the expense of their romance.

This book examines *La La Land*'s development, style, and reception. Drawing on extensive personal interviews with director Damien Chazelle, composer Justin Hurwitz, choreographer Mandy Moore, and lyricists Benj Pasek and Justin Paul, I explore *La La Land*'s aesthetic approach to the film musical genre, particularly its simultaneous engagement with and subversion of the classic Hollywood musical's stylistic and narrative expectations. I delve into the film's depiction of jazz, which is a central focus of the story. In considering the reception of the film, I focus particularly on the ways in which the critical response reflects broader cultural expectations and understandings of the film musical and its continued appeal for 21st-century audiences.

Each chapter delves into various aspects of *La La Land*'s style and reception, placing it in its historical, aesthetic, and cultural context. The first chapter traces the film from its early development to the final version, beginning with the start of Chazelle and Hurwitz's collaboration on Chazelle's college thesis film, *Guy and Madeline on a Park Bench*. I describe the aesthetic preoccupations that led them to develop a "realist musical," the evolution of the project, and the factors that led to the final version of the screenplay, stressing the collaborative nature of the film while also pointing to the auteurist tendencies across Chazelle's work. Chapter 2 delves into the specific references to Golden Age film musicals, the source of many of the film's joyous moments. I analyze audiovisual references to *The Umbrellas of Cherbourg, Singin' in the Rain, An American in Paris*, and others, arguing that this intertextuality reflexively places *La La Land* in dialogue with its own genre's history. These overt references act as a form of homage, but they also function as nostalgia for an older era and style of filmmaking. This nostalgia, in turn, is a crucial element of the film's mythmaking. At the same time, I show how the creative team infused the film's references with a degree of cynicism that runs in tension with its nostalgic project. Chapter 3 explores how the traditional style and story of the film are updated for contemporary sensibilities, particularly the creative team's approach to realism. The most drastic departure from Hollywood musical conventions is perhaps the depiction of the leading couple's relationship, but the use of contemporary camerawork is another means of modernizing the classic form. I place *La La Land*'s audiovisual style in the broader context of trends in contemporary Hollywood musicals, and consider how the tensions between virtuosity, realism, and technology play out in the film.

Jazz is central to *La La Land*'s story. Sebastian's definition of jazz is myopic, narrowly fixed in a particular moment in the genre's history. He believes he is "selling out" when he goes on tour with Keith, a musician who, depending on one's perspective, is either reinventing jazz for a wider, more popular audience or bastardizing the genre. The film's portrayal of jazz is the aspect that has received the most extensive discussion and debate, particularly surrounding the intersections of race and genre in the jazz subplot. In Chapter 4, I delve into *La La Land*'s ambivalence about jazz's stylistic boundaries, and how its depiction of the genre connects to the film's broader racial representation. Chapter 5 examines the film's reception. Its initial near-unanimous critical praise was followed by a backlash on the part of some critics and viewers, reflecting the polarizing nature of its approach to reviving and contemporizing the film musical genre. I further argue that the film's reception was mediated by a shift in national mood in response to current events right around its premiere (mainly the 2016 presidential election), as well as cultural shifts in Hollywood around racial and gender representation.

Indeed, in the way it reflects its appreciation for Hollywood's past while engaging with the film musical's role in the present, *La La Land* can tell us a lot about its cultural moment. It was both singular in its aesthetic approach to the film musical genre and representative of broader aesthetic and cultural discussions occurring around the time of its premiere. By exploring the range of stylistic and cultural debates that *La La Land* prompted, we can learn a great deal about the continued relevance of the film musical in the 21st century.

1

The Development of a "Realist Musical"

The Chazelle–Hurwitz Collaboration

It's a story made for Hollywood. Two college roommates move to Los Angeles upon graduation to pursue their dreams, one as a writer-director and the other as a composer. They encounter challenges along the way, but after years of persistence and a few lucky breaks, they achieve their goal with a film about making it in the entertainment industry, which becomes a massive critical and commercial success. It sounds almost like a cliché, the stuff of classic mid-century backstage musicals like *Babes in Arms* (1939) or *Singin' in the Rain* (1952).

Indeed, as filmmaker Damien Chazelle and composer Justin Hurwitz describe their experiences leading up to the success of *La La Land*, their story could be its own Hollywood screenplay.[1] In 2004, Chazelle and Hurwitz became roommates at Harvard. The two found that they shared many aesthetic preoccupations, and they encouraged each other to work hard on improving their craft, Chazelle as a filmmaker and Hurwitz as a composer. After graduating, they tried their luck in Hollywood. They toiled to pay the bills, living in cramped apartments with multiple roommates and experiencing a number of disappointments and setbacks along the way. After another film brought them critical attention, their dream project was finally picked up by a major studio, and they suddenly saw their vision come together on a massive scale, with a huge budget and major movie stars. Only a few years after they moved to L.A., their success was exemplified by their triumph at the Oscars: Hurwitz won two for *La La Land* (Best Original Score and Best Song), and Chazelle became the youngest Best Director winner of all time. *La La Land* became the most acclaimed original film musical in decades.

This narrative of Chazelle and Hurwitz's path to Hollywood success is particularly interesting given the parallels with the narrative of *La La Land* itself. In both the film and the story of its creation, a pair of individuals works hard, each supporting the other's pursuit of a creative vision at all costs. In

La La Land. Hannah Lewis, Oxford University Press. © Oxford University Press 2024.
DOI: 10.1093/9780197682616.003.0002

the film, Mia and Seb pursue their dream careers with very few sacrifices to their creative goals, but the sacrifice comes in their personal lives: in order to support each other, they end their relationship. In real life, Chazelle and Hurwitz may have made personal sacrifices to pursue their dreams, but their close friendship and collaboration remained a constant. Their partnership is reminiscent of high-profile collaborators on stage and screen, like Hal Prince and Stephen Sondheim, Tim Burton and Danny Elfman, Wes Anderson and Alexandre Desplat, or their idols, Jacques Demy and Michel Legrand. To this date, neither Chazelle nor Hurwitz has made a film without the other, from Chazelle's college senior thesis, *Guy and Madeline on a Park Bench* (2009); to *Whiplash* (2014), their first major Hollywood success, about a jazz drummer and his abusive teacher; to *La La Land*; to their biopic of astronaut Neil Armstrong, *First Man* (2018); and, most recently, their period drama *Babylon* (2022), which depicts Hollywood during the transition to synchronized sound.[2] Although each project has different stylistic and thematic traits, all of their films deal in some way with people working toward a goal and the price they pay to achieve it.[3] And three of their films center around music and musicians, especially jazz musicians. In many respects, the friends' artistic journey is a case of life imitating art.

Of course, Chazelle and Hurwitz's path to success was more complicated, marked by a combination of important connections, hard work, and lucky breaks. Even so, the ability of two friends to realize their vision in a successful Hollywood film at such a young age, with so little experience in the industry, is highly unusual; even more unusual is the stylistic consistency they managed to maintain from their initial idea to the final product. Nevertheless, the success of *La La Land* was contingent upon effective collaboration with a number of individuals—producers, actors, lyricists, the music director, and the choreographer, to name a few—all of whom made important decisions that impacted the final version of the film.

This chapter traces the development of *La La Land* from Chazelle and Hurwitz's first collaboration at Harvard to the final version that premiered in 2016. Drawing on press accounts and my own personal interviews with Chazelle, Hurwitz, and other members of the creative team, I recount how *La La Land* developed and evolved, from both logistical and aesthetic standpoints, considering the factors that led to the final version of the screenplay, songs, and story. Throughout, I stress the collaborative nature of the film's development, while also pointing to the auteurist tendencies across Chazelle's work—his stylistic control over the various aspects of his films that are recognizable as distinctly his own—and the importance of Hurwitz's music in sonically marking his collaborator's individual style.

The Beginning of the Collaboration

Chazelle, the son of two college professors, grew up in Princeton, New Jersey. He states that he always knew he wanted to be a filmmaker: he had a "one-track mind growing up, so it was basically film or bust . . . film was the constant."[4] At first, he hated musicals; he was turned off by actors breaking into song and by the narrative interruption of musical numbers. It was in late high school and his early college years studying film at Harvard that he became interested in the genre. According to Chazelle, he was finally drawn to film musicals through an "avant-garde perspective": he suddenly found "that I was liking the exact same thing that I had resisted before, which was the idea of a . . . sustained narrative getting halted or redirected in some way; the digressive idea of a musical number suddenly really appealed to me."[5] He quickly "made up for lost time," diving deep into the genre and watching countless classic Hollywood musicals.

French New Wave director Jacques Demy's musicals *Les Parapluies de Cherbourg* [*The Umbrellas of Cherbourg*] (1964) and *Les Demoiselles de Rochefort* [*The Young Ladies of Rochefort*] (1967) made a particularly strong impression on Chazelle. He describes his introduction to Demy's films as a revelation, as he realized that "a musical can be more lifelike than I thought."[6] Demy's films are their own reinterpretations of the film musical genre, from the perspective of the French New Wave. Full of visual and narrative references to classic Hollywood musicals, they also subvert audience expectations of the genre. *Les Parapluies de Cherbourg*, for instance, is filmed in a rich, saturated Technicolor associated with 1950s Hollywood musicals, but unlike a typical Hollywood musical, it is through-sung like an opera, with a score by Michel Legrand that combines jazz idioms with full symphonic orchestrations.[7] Demy uses a larger-than-life style to tell a story with serious contemporary commentary on the impact of the Algerian War in France, premarital sex and pregnancy, and economic instability. The film's romantic protagonists do not end up together, though they poignantly encounter each other briefly at the end.[8] *Les Demoiselles de Rochefort* addresses some of the same serious themes as Demy's earlier musical, but it has more of a traditional Hollywood musical structure, with distinct numbers. Demy's films opened the door to the film musical genre for Chazelle at a time when he was also becoming interested in the New Wave experimentation of filmmakers like Jean-Luc Godard. Through Demy, he was drawn to the very films that Demy referenced and subverted, finding them to be the "commercial experimental movies that I had never known about, couching the avant-garde in populist terms."[9] He also appreciated the way that, despite how stylized Demy's films were, they seemed to mirror life, especially in *Cherbourg's* "reunion non-reunion" of the lovers at the end of the film.

The only interest that "threatened film for the throne" for Chazelle was music. His father, who was born in France but moved to the United States as a young adult—in part, Chazelle suspects, "because of how much he loved American music"—played guitar in the house frequently while Chazelle was growing up, and influenced his strong interest in music.[10] Chazelle also played jazz drums in high school in a competitive program. This background led to his interest in writing and directing films focused on music and musicians.

Hurwitz, who was born in California but grew up mostly in Wisconsin, began his musical training at a young age. He started piano lessons at age six and became interested in composing at age ten, when his parents bought him a synthesizer and a sequencer, a "little box" that allowed him to layer tracks.[11] He realized he loved composing much more than he liked practicing the piano: "It always felt like a chore, whereas composing . . . was completely different. The hours would just disappear."[12] He studied composition at Harvard, taking classes in traditional music theory and orchestration. He describes his music theory courses as being particularly influential for his developing voice as a composer, especially the ways tonal harmony served as the basis both for classical art music and for popular music genres like jazz. According to Hurwitz, his tonal theory teacher would bring in jazz standards, noting jokingly (and somewhat reductively) how the chord progressions were "the same thing as Bach. They just add sevenths."[13]

Chazelle and Hurwitz met during their freshman year at Harvard. They played in a local indie band, Chester French—Chazelle on drums and Hurwitz on keyboard—and realized they had a common interest in film. The two soon quit the band and became roommates their sophomore year. They appreciated each other's ambition and work ethic; they were both "obsessive," according to Hurwitz, and comfortable working with nonstop, laser focus on their own projects.[14] According to both Chazelle and Hurwitz, the two spent their years as roommates keeping a low profile, working tirelessly on their own to improve their craft, and "egg[ing] each other on" to work harder.[15] At the same time, they bonded over films and over their increasingly overlapping musical tastes.

Chazelle introduced Hurwitz to the films of Demy, which proved to be the perfect point of entry into the film musical genre for him as well. Hurwitz was already interested in film music, drawn to "tuneful, memorable, emotional" scores written by the likes of John Williams.[16] But Demy's films, and Legrand's music in particular, became a strong source of inspiration for Hurwitz; he was drawn to Legrand's distinctive style, which married jazz harmonic and rhythmic idioms with full, lush orchestration. Hurwitz frequently cites Legrand as an influence, but it is worth noting that Legrand's compositions were participating in a broader musical phenomenon that John Howland calls "luxe pop," a merging of popular musical styles with lush string orchestrations.[17] With roots in Tin Pan Alley, big band, and interwar Broadway and Hollywood, luxe pop remained salient throughout the 20th century in genres from big band to R&B and soul to hip-hop, embraced by musicians as diverse as the Beach Boys, Frank Sinatra, Isaac Hayes, and Jay-Z. Hurwitz's musical style is therefore influenced not only by Legrand, but also by Legrand's luxe pop predecessors and contemporaries. Nevertheless, in their first film collaboration, *Guy and Madeline on a Park Bench*, Chazelle and Hurwitz self-consciously drew on Demy's and Legrand's influences.

Guy and Madeline on a Park Bench

Guy and Madeline was Chazelle's senior thesis film, a low-budget and experimental depiction of a failed romantic relationship through film musical tropes. At Harvard, Chazelle's courses in the Department of Film and Visual Studies were strongly focused on fly-on-the-wall, *cinéma verité*–style filmmaking. At the same time, he wanted to explore what he calls his "academic theories of the musical," and he became interested in seeing what would happen if he linked the two practices. In a 2009 *IndieWire* interview, Chazelle claimed that he was "less interested in the theatrical aspects of the musical and more in the vision of the world musicals present: a world in which there's a very fine line between conversation and song, between casually walking down the street and tap-dancing down it."[18] He shot the film in black and white on a 16 mm camera and with a budget of $60,000.[19] He asked Hurwitz to write the music, and he agreed; Chazelle claims that if Hurwitz had said no, he probably would have abandoned the idea of making a musical. For Chazelle, *Guy and Madeline* was the duo's "laboratory" for working out their stylistic preoccupations that would culminate in *La La Land*; in particular, it was their first chance to experiment with the idea of a "realist musical."

Guy and Madeline grew into a larger project beyond a senior thesis, but one that was reliant on the creative team's Harvard network for funding and personnel: over the course of shooting, Chazelle undertook fundraising in order to afford film stock and processing, and he also received an Artist Development Fund from Harvard.[20] The film became a critical success at festivals, giving the pair a tangible (albeit modest) filmography before they moved to Hollywood to embark on their respective careers.[21]

In *Guy and Madeline*, both Chazelle and Hurwitz experimented with stylistic and narrative choices that would strongly inform *La La Land*. Both films, for instance, focus on a romance that does not end happily. *Guy and Madeline* depicts the relationship between the title characters, following each of them in the days and months after their breakup. They briefly reunite at the end of the film long enough to consider whether they should move on or rekindle their romance. Both films also subvert expectations for the larger-than-life, artificial style in film musicals by bringing more naturalistic aspects into the genre. For *Guy and Madeline*, Chazelle wanted to make a musical that felt lifelike, "really small and intimate, and kind of ordinary, about ordinary people," incorporating musical numbers into a film that otherwise feels like a documentary.[22] He used a hand-held camera to follow characters around, and much of the dialogue was improvised by the actors, giving the film a spontaneous quality. Just like *La La Land*, the film also focuses on a jazz musician: Guy, an African American trumpet player, played by the real-life jazz musician Jason Palmer, who performed frequently at Wally's jazz club in Boston. The film also explicitly references older musicals, particularly those of Demy. As a direct homage, the title characters share names with two of the lead characters in *Les Parapluies de Cherbourg*.

The film also gave Hurwitz the opportunity to experiment with an aspect of his compositional style that later became important for *La La Land*: his incorporation of classic jazz harmonies with lush orchestration. For *Guy and Madeline*, he sought to emulate 1930s and 1940s jazz standards. The influence of Legrand's style is also apparent, particularly in his frequent use of sequences and circles of fifths, and in his luxe pop blending of American vernacular musical elements with symphonic orchestration.

Furthermore, with *Guy and Madeline*, Chazelle and Hurwitz also established a working method that has remained consistent through their subsequent collaborations. According to Chazelle, Hurwitz would send him countless demos, which Chazelle would provide feedback on; they would then continue to exchange demos, going back and forth until they built to something they both liked.[23] Just as in each subsequent collaboration, Chazelle gave Hurwitz the time and space to compose at his own pace and gave music a privileged role in the film's conception. Hurwitz also orchestrated his own music for *Guy and Madeline*. He did not hear his own orchestrations until he went to hear the Bratislava Symphony Orchestra record the score during a single four-hour session. According to Hurwitz, it was a formative experience: although he admits there were technical problems with the score, since it was the first time he had ever heard his own orchestrations played back, there was also a "certain inspired quality" to the colors in the score because he did not bring in any preconceived notions of how his orchestrations were supposed to sound.[24]

Both Chazelle's realist audiovisual approach and Hurwitz's jazz-classic-inspired compositional style are on full display in the song "Love in the Fall." The song occurs at a party in a recording studio after a group of musicians has finished cutting an album, where the fly-on-the-wall camera captures multiple conversations, mostly unintelligible amidst the din of the gathering. One man in close-up begins talking about love in the fall, a walking bass line coming in underneath his dialogue. It is unclear at first if this is just a coincidence—the band could be warming up as the man talks to a fellow partygoer—but it soon becomes clear the man is speaking in rhyme, which serves as a transition into the song.[25] We now see a jazz combo playing onscreen as the man sings. The song emulates the style of classic jazz standards of the 1940s, a reference reinforced by the man's vocal performance (Musical Example 1.1). The man then begins tap dancing and invites a woman to join him. The whole number was filmed in a single take, with all sound recorded live, and the camera travels frequently, using a series of whip pans (rapid pan shots that blur the picture as the camera moves) to alternate between the dancing couple, surrounded by the rest of the partygoers, and Guy, playing trumpet in the next room (Figures 1.1a–b). The shaky camera and the seemingly spontaneous reaction of the partygoers (acting as

Musical Example 1.1 "Love in the Fall" (excerpt), *Guy and Madeline on a Park Bench* (2009) (my transcription)

the diegetic audience), combined with the virtuosic tap dancing, created the blend of realism and the ebullience and *joie de vivre* of the film musical that Chazelle was aiming for. He would adapt a very similar filming technique for "Herman's Habit" in *La La Land*, complete with the whip pans between jazz musicians and dancing audience members.

There are some crucial differences between *Guy and Madeline* and *La La Land*, some more immediately apparent than others. As the work of a young and inexperienced filmmaker and composer, *Guy and Madeline* is less polished than *La La Land*, owing to their inexperience and to the much smaller budget, but it is also more experimental in spirit. The former purposely exploits the low-budget feel of the black-and-white, handheld camera, while the latter is in lavish, color-saturated CinemaScope.[26] *Guy and Madeline* is notably more diverse in its casting, with Black and Latina leads (Jason Palmer and Desirée Garcia), contrasting with *La La Land*'s white leading couple Ryan Gosling and Emma Stone, a casting choice with significant implications for the film's story and reception (discussed more fully in Chapter 4). But the stylistic and narrative aspects shared between *Guy and Madeline* and *La La Land* also reflect a clear set of auteurist priorities on the part of Chazelle. According to Chazelle, the central conceit of *Guy and Madeline*'s style—"How lifelike can you make a musical?"—and its subversion of film musical expectations remained a core theme for him in *La La Land* as well. *Guy and Madeline* premiered at the Tribeca Film Festival in 2009 and was screened at a number of other smaller film festivals internationally.[27] Its success at film festivals gave the pair the legitimacy to embark on careers in Hollywood. Moreover, its content and style gave them material to adapt when they began to pursue the possibility of making a film musical on a bigger budget. Chazelle was eager to explore some of the same theoretical concepts, but in saturated color and CinemaScope.

(a)

(b)

Figures 1.1a–b "Love in the Fall," *Guy and Madeline on a Park Bench* (2009)

Chazelle and Hurwitz in Hollywood: The Early Development of *La La Land*

The next few years—from the duo's move to Hollywood to the time *La La Land* was picked up by a major studio—can be understood either as a triumph against all odds, thanks to the persistence and single-mindedness of Chazelle and Hurwitz, or as a relatively swift success, thanks to luck, connections, and the pair's ability to articulate a clear vision to investors. Chazelle has discussed the formative experience of "imagining L.A. in your head, which is mainly how you have seen it in movies, and then coming to L.A. and the ways it lives up to those stereotypes, the ways it doesn't, and the ways in which it surprises you."[28] But as two relative unknowns who were new to Hollywood, they initially had trouble finding anyone willing to finance the production of an original musical, which is a costly, logistically complicated undertaking. At the time, Hollywood was experiencing a resurgence of film musical adaptations of stage productions, including *Hairspray* (2007), *Mamma Mia!* (2008), and *Les Misérables* (2012), but these films had name recognition to help them at the box office. With *Moulin Rouge!* (2001) as a notable exception, very few high-profile original movie musicals had been produced (apart from animated films) since the 1990s, and certainly not by Hollywood newcomers.

Chazelle paid the bills as a writer-for-hire, and Hurwitz found a job writing for television comedies, but both maintained the express goal of collaborating on a film musical. Chazelle described how, on the advice of an executive at Focus Features, he aimed to write a musical "on a bigger scale [than *Guy and Madeline*]. Not big, but the next step up."[29] In its early conceptions, the project, originally titled *So Long, Jupiter*, shared many similarities with *Guy and Madeline*: a focus on classic jazz both in the narrative and in the musical style, a musician protagonist, a relationship that doesn't work out, and a "lifelike" approach to the musical genre, or an intentional blend of realism and fantasy. Over the course of various versions, they made the important decision to set it in Los Angeles: Chazelle describes how Boston "felt like a square, black-and-white" city, whereas L.A. felt "bright, sometimes blindingly bright, sunlit, outdoors, widescreen, flat, horizon, and very saturated color."[30] Chazelle wrote many different versions of the script over the years, but they all shared a few common features, most notably a bittersweet ending. Hurwitz composed "Mia & Sebastian's Theme" early in their brainstorming process (although it was not given that name until later), but none of the other initial songs from earlier drafts remained in the final version.[31]

In 2011, after Chazelle and Hurwitz had been developing their ideas for about a year, producers Fred Berger and Jordan Horowitz took interest in their project.[32] Berger and Horowitz were young producers, both of whom had also recently moved to L.A. and decided to strike it on their own.[33] Impressed with Chazelle's strong articulation of his vision for the film, they became important supporters of the project over the course of its six-year development. Berger and Horowitz took the script to Focus Features with a proposed $1 million budget. However, Focus pushed for some substantial changes, including changing the male lead from a jazz pianist to a rock musician and dropping the bittersweet ending.[34] Ultimately, the script went into turnaround, meaning the producers could pursue the project at another studio. But the situation soon changed: Chazelle's next film, *Whiplash*, significantly increased his name recognition and clout.

Whiplash

After what seemed like a dead end with his musical script, Chazelle turned his attention to a project that would be a less risky investment for producers, and it became his first major Hollywood success. *Whiplash* is about Andrew Neiman (played by Miles Teller), a first-year jazz drummer at the prestigious fictional Shaffer Conservatory in New York City, and his abusive teacher, Terence Fletcher (played by J. K. Simmons). Chazelle based the screenplay loosely on his own experience with a demanding teacher during his years playing jazz drums in high school, but he portrayed the abuse to the extreme: Fletcher verbally and physically attacks Andrew, driving him to the point of a near mental breakdown. The film's abuse narrative mirrors that of jazz drummer Buddy Rich, who was famous for his temper and physical and verbal violence; throughout the film, Andrew idolizes Rich, seeming to believe that abuse is justified if it results in musical greatness. Though the film does not overtly condone this kind of abuse, and portrays Fletcher as inappropriate and unhinged, its final musical performance seems to suggest that perhaps the ends justify the means.[35]

After the critical success of a short film of the same name that Chazelle wrote and directed, he found investors to produce a feature-length version. Hurwitz collaborated with big band arranger Tim Simonec, writing several diegetic pieces for the big band in the film, as well as the nondiegetic score. Though *Whiplash* is not a traditional musical, it still reveals certain common aspects of Chazelle's style, particularly in its questioning what sacrifices are necessary to excel at one's dream, in Chazelle's experimentation with different visual editing styles for musical performances, and in its focus on jazz and its place in contemporary life from the perspective of white jazz musicians (see Chapter 4). For Hurwitz, it gave him valuable experience writing and orchestrating for big band.

A critical triumph, *Whiplash* was nominated for several Academy Awards, including Best Picture. The film was seen as Chazelle's breakout success, putting him on the map as a Hollywood wunderkind. As Chazelle cheekily claims, "What really changed, what really opened appetites, was not that musicals suddenly became seen as commercial. It was that we made *Whiplash*. And that suddenly made us a little more palatable . . . for anyone with money in Hollywood who wanted to see some of that money back."[36] Suddenly, multiple studios were interested in producing Chazelle's next film. Ultimately Lionsgate signed on to the project, and Chazelle and Hurwitz scaled up to a $30 million budget. By 2015, it was described in the press as "an old fashioned musical set in contemporary Los Angeles . . . center[ing] on a love story between a jazz pianist and an aspiring actress."[37]

The Film Takes Form

After the film was backed by Lionsgate, the evolution of *La La Land* both reinforces Chazelle and Hurwitz's single-minded drive to realize their vision, a vision that remained relatively stable over the course of the film's production, and reveals the collaborative nature of the film and the important influence of the actors and other members of the creative team—producers, music director, lyricists, and choreographer—over the final version. Music director Marius de Vries joined *La La Land* in April 2014, becoming the first member of the production team hired for the film.[38] Born in London, de Vries had a background as a producer and programmer for a number of famous popular music acts like David Bowie, U2, Madonna, Björk, and Rufus Wainwright. He composed the music for Baz Luhrmann's 1996 film *Romeo + Juliet,* and he later worked as music director for Luhrmann's postmodern film musical *Moulin Rouge!* When de Vries joined the *La La Land* team, Hurwitz had written many of the melodies, but there were no lyrics, and the overall musical shape of the film had yet to be developed. According to de Vries, his role on the film was "custodial," helping to nurture Hurwitz's musical vision, as well as "nuts-and-bolts," working through the logistics of getting it made. He also worked closely with the performers to help "elicit the best performance" possible.[39] As a trusted insider in Hollywood, de Vries proved to be an important advocate for Chazelle and Hurwitz's overall musical vision, while overseeing many of the technical aspects of music production. He claims that one of the main challenges of the film was to "respect all the influences [Chazelle and Hurwitz] were paying homage to," while also trying to create a musical that would sound contemporary.[40] For de Vries, this meant executing the music recording meticulously, using modern recording technologies but keeping technological intervention as inaudible as possible.

At this early stage, the songs were still missing lyrics, but musical theater songwriting duo Benj Pasek and Justin Paul soon joined the team as lyricists. Pasek and Paul, who later became known for their Broadway hit *Dear Evan Hansen* (2015) and their music and lyrics for the film *The Greatest Showman* (2017), began writing musical theater together when they were classmates at the University of Michigan. As collaborators, Pasek and Paul had a lot in common with Chazelle and Hurwitz: they met each other and began collaborating in college, and they shared a love of movie musicals. Although they have worked extensively for the stage, Pasek and Paul describe how their first encounter with musical theater was through film, particularly Disney animated films like *The Little Mermaid* (1989) and *Aladdin* (1992).[41] Chazelle, Hurwitz, Pasek, and Paul met, first over the phone and then over dinner, to discuss their potential collaboration for *La La Land*. As an "audition" for the project, Pasek and Paul wrote lyrics for "City of Stars," which was at the time only called "Ballad." The four men hit it off: Paul suggests they were "cut from the same cloth" in their interest in making new art while paying homage to and drawing influence from earlier musicals. They connected over their common interests and found a natural aesthetic fit in the lyrics that Pasek and Paul had written for Hurwitz's melody.[42]

By the time Pasek and Paul joined the project, the music had been mostly written, and they mainly had to write lyrics to Hurwitz's existing melodies. Pasek describes how this was an atypical working process for him and Paul—they usually write both music and lyrics—but they aimed to set lyrics that felt natural and "like they can work for the character," that "[advanced] the plot when necessary," and that did not get in the way of the emotional arc of the music, making it feel "like it was made in tandem."[43] They would often have to "reverse engineer" a lyric, looking for exactly the right number of syllables or scansion that fit with the melody, but occasionally they would ask Hurwitz to adapt his melodies slightly to fit their lyrics. Throughout, they aimed to match the combination of joy and melancholy that Chazelle and Hurwitz had already developed in their script and music.

Choreographer Mandy Moore also played an important role in shaping the final film. Known for her work choreographing for reality television shows like *So You Think You Can Dance* and *Dancing with the Stars*, Moore moved to Los Angeles when she was eighteen to train at EDGE Performing Arts Center.[44] She grew up watching MGM musicals and performing in community theater, but upon arriving in Los Angeles, she felt like "this weird musical theater person in L.A.," a theater person in a commercial dance world.[45] Although she has choreographed for stage and screen, she particularly likes working with the camera, and she enjoys working in a variety of genres and styles, as long as a project combines movement and storytelling.

If the request from the producers had been for a period piece, Moore claims she would not have been the right person for the job. But many of the films and styles being referenced were a nostalgic part of her childhood, which gave her an emotional connection to the material. Moore describes how, before she signed on to the project, Lionsgate "had basically met with every choreographer in L.A."[46] But when she met with Chazelle, Berger, and Horowitz, she found they all just "clicked." As an "audition," she was asked to bring in ideas for "Someone in the Crowd"—which she described as being a take on *West Side Story*'s "I Feel Pretty" but "a little more brash"— and "Planetarium." While casting was being finalized, Moore brainstormed and met with Chazelle for what she called "download meetings," where he would describe his vision for different numbers and share video clips that inspired him or that suggested a particular mood or idea he wanted to emulate.[47]

When the lead actors came on board, the shape of the film changed in more significant ways based on the actors' understanding of their characters. Chazelle wanted his main characters to be relatable; as a result, he chose to cast "actors who would learn to sing or dance, rather than singers or dancers who learned to act."[48] Many actors were considered for both leads, including Miles Teller (who had starred in *Whiplash*) for the role of Sebastian and Emma Watson for the role of Mia.[49] Eventually, Ryan Gosling and Emma Stone signed on. Chazelle claims that he had "dreamed of [Stone] early on" and "she seemed kind of perfect," but that it was a fantasy idea until they had a major studio behind the project.[50] Similarly, Berger suggested that "it was always Ryan Gosling and Emma Stone in our heads," but that "it was always an impossibility that we would get them, also in our heads, because they were just so perfect that we never let ourselves believe they would do this film. So we were always looking for who were the best replicas of them."[51] Stone and Gosling had already developed an onscreen chemistry, having previously starred together in the romantic comedy *Crazy, Stupid, Love* (2011) and the thriller *Gangster Squad* (2013).

By this time, veteran musical theater and movie producer Marc Platt had signed on as producer. He had previously worked with Gosling on three other films, and he later suggested that one of his key roles was to act as a bridge between Chazelle, who had not previously worked with such high-profile movie stars, and Stone and Gosling, who were new to the film musical genre.[52] Although both actors had little previous formal singing or dance training, Stone had recently starred as Sally Bowles in the Broadway revival of *Cabaret*, and Gosling was part of the indie rock duo Dead Man's Bones, contributing vocals and a number of musical instruments on their 2009 album. For the film, the two went through several weeks of intensive vocal and dance training. Moore exposed them to ballroom, tap, and jazz, aiming to get them comfortable with movement before introducing them to the film's specific choreography.[53] Stone also studied Pilates to help with her alignment, and Gosling took piano lessons (becoming proficient enough not to require a hand double).[54]

Chazelle and the other members of the creative team made changes to adapt the roles for the two stars' skills and strengths. Chazelle describes the conversations he had with the actors about different aspects of their characters, sitting in a room "for hours on end" talking "about everything about the characters and backstory,"[55] and explains that they made some changes according to how Stone and Gosling believed each of their characters would behave. For instance, Gosling suggested that Seb should have the concrete goal of opening his own jazz club, rather than the vaguer aim of achieving success as a jazz musician, and Stone proposed the idea that Mia develop the sign for Seb's club, which would visually symbolize their impact on each other's careers.[56] Chazelle also describes how, to add spontaneity to the dialogue, he would sit in a room with the actors and have them improvise a scene.[57] Unlike the looser spontaneity of the improvised dialogue in *Guy and Madeline*, however, Chazelle would write down the improvisations and ask the actors to internalize them, so every aspect of a scene was pre-determined before shooting. Since many of the scenes were going to be shot as continuous takes, each one had to be "a dance" that would be "blocked and choreographed, focus pulled, camera here, actor there, every single inch of it. . . . So it had to be timed properly."

Hurwitz also made some adjustments to his music to suit the actors' voices. He describes that the different vocal ranges of the two actors made the duets challenging. In "City of Stars," for instance, Gosling wanted to sing in the low end of his range, but setting the song low enough for his preference would have required Stone to jump an octave, making her vocals too breathy. For "A Lovely Night," after the actors could not agree on a key, Hurwitz added a four-bar modulation so that the two could sing in different keys.[58] Hurwitz also described a specific instance where Gosling changed the melody he had written. The opening verse melody for "A Lovely Night" includes a some-what angular melody with disjunct motion that leads to the octave above the starting note. Gosling was resistant to the phrase, instead replacing the melody with a more *sprechstimme*-quality line. Hurwitz and Gosling argued back and forth about the melody of the song all the way through post-production. Ultimately, Hurwitz convinced Gosling to re-record the melody for the lyrics "a silver shine that stretches to the sea" (Musical Example 1.2a), a more poetic line that merits more complex melodic material, and Gosling's version of the melody remains for the line "what a shame those two are you and me" (Musical Example 1.2b), which captures the more colloquial or con-versational nature of the lyrics in that moment. Pasek and Paul also made changes to the lyrics at the actors' requests: according to de Vries, the lyrics to "A Lovely Night" were complete a month before shooting, but when Stone and Gosling read them, they felt they were too "acerbic" for their characters, and Pasek and Paul wrote new lyrics.[59]

All of Chazelle's collaborators have remarked that he articulated a very clear vision for the film throughout pre-production. For instance, Moore describes the collaborative process with Chazelle as a "back-and-forth," while at the same time, he knew exactly what he wanted with each number. According to Moore, although he never dictated specific choreography, he would indicate the visual effect he wanted in a scene, which would inform her choreographic choices. For instance, on the location scout for "Someone in the Crowd," Chazelle created a mock shot with his iPhone where he narrated the action and movement of the scene as he walked through the space.[60] Similarly, Hurwitz describes how Chazelle had the whole movie in

(a)

Musical Examples 1.2a–b "A Lovely Night" (excerpts), Gosling's vocal parts, *La La Land* (2016)

A Lovely Night
from LA LA LAND
Music by Justin Hurwitz
Lyrics by Benj Pasek & Justin Paul
© 2016 Justin Hurwitz Music (BMI), Warner-Tamerlane Publishing Corp. (BMI), administered by Warner-Tamerlane Publishing Corp. (BMI), and B Lion Music (BMI) administered by Songs Of Universal, Inc. (BMI)/Pick In A Pinch Music (ASCAP), breathelike music (ASCAP), WC Music Corp. (ASCAP) administered by WC Music Corp. (ASCAP) and A Lion Music (ASCAP) administered by Universal Music Corp. (ASCAP)
This arrangement © 2016 Justin Hurwitz Music (BMI), Warner-Tamerlane Publishing Corp. (BMI), administered by Warner-Tamerlane Publishing Corp. (BMI), and B Lion Music (BMI) administered by Songs Of Universal, Inc. (BMI)/Pick In A Pinch Music (ASCAP), breathelike music (ASCAP), WC Music Corp. (ASCAP) administered by WC Music Corp. (ASCAP) and A Lion Music (ASCAP) administered by Universal Music Corp. (ASCAP)
All Rights Reserved   Used by Permission
Reprinted by permission of Hal Leonard LLC

his head, and could tell if a musical section was four seconds too long and needed to be cut, or if a scene needed more music for an actor to move from one place to another. This kind of specificity allowed Hurwitz to make musical edits during the demo phase, rather than requiring extensive editing of the final mix.[61] By all accounts, it seems Chazelle's vision was fully backed by the studio, enabling him to maintain tight control over most aspects of the film. Producer Marc Platt said that one of his primary aims as producer was "protecting [Chazelle's] vision," particularly against outside pressures to conform to existing Hollywood practices and conventional wisdom about what would assure box office success.[62]

Hurwitz, on the other hand, describes having to fight tooth and nail against the studio to allow him to realize his compositional vision. He claims that when Chazelle demanded to work with him, that producers and executives would "reluctantly accept" him but remained "very suspicious" of him, owing to his lack of name recognition and experience in Hollywood.[63] Even though Chazelle was "confident in [him]," "loyal," and "persuasive with the studios," Hurwitz felt that his position as composer was constantly under threat. When Interscope was signed on as the record label partner, for instance, the head of soundtracks wanted to bring Interscope-signed artists into the project to collaborate on some songs; Chazelle refused because he worried the film would become a "made-by-committee musical." Even when Hurwitz's contract was officially signed, he claims that Interscope and Lionsgate would try to push him to take meetings with other songwriters, suggesting that sharing a writing credit with someone like Justin Timberlake—even if Timberlake only contributed one word to a song—would be a huge boon for Hurwitz's career.[64] According to Hurwitz, once Platt was signed on as producer, the situation improved because Platt "knew how to advocate for the artists" and served as an effective politician between the artists and executives. Hurwitz and Chazelle managed to hold firm, and Hurwitz was the sole composer and songwriter (with the exception of his collaboration with John Legend for "Light a Fire," discussed in Chapter 4).

But according to Hurwitz, the challenges did not stop there. He was continuously pressured for not having what the studio deemed a "hit song," and he was frequently asked, "Where's your 'Let It Go' song?" (referring to the hit from the 2013 Disney animated film *Frozen*). He describes having to fight the studio once again when it came to his orchestrations: he wanted to do them all himself, which is very unusual for a film composer, and he was pressured to bring in collaborators who could at least "check [his] work." He persisted and completed all orchestrations himself, with the assistance of the music department in creating realistic mockups before recording.[65] De Vries acted as a strong advocate; he claims that by the time he joined the project, Hurwitz's orchestrations were well on their way—indeed, "pretty much at genius level" despite Hurwitz's inexperience—and he felt it was part of his job description to "nurture and protect that process . . . under the scrutiny of outsiders."[66] Hurwitz describes the moment in the first recording session when "the mood in the room changed," and Hurwitz himself "physiologically [felt] this relief," after the orchestra played the first few bars of "Another Day of Sun," and it became clear to everyone in the room that his orchestrations were going to be effective.[67]

Even with Chazelle's and Hurwitz's persistence in maintaining their vision for the project as other collaborators came in, they did end up making some more substantial changes to certain musical numbers, both during pre-production and after the film had been shot, based on external feedback. For instance, "Someone in the Crowd" was supposed to be twice as long, with an additional verse and chorus. The scene was filmed as one long continuous take, which would follow the roommates around the apartment, float out the window, and catch them on the stairs going down to the courtyard before they walk to Mia's car. But with so much attention focused on the roommates, audiences in test screens were not as invested in Mia at that point in the film as everyone would have liked. So, they sacrificed the virtuosic camera shot and cut out the second verse and chorus, opting instead to insert a separate shot of Mia looking up at the ceiling as she decides whether or not to attend the party.

Chazelle and Hurwitz both describe working with several versions of the opening of the film, one of which eliminated "Another Day of Sun" entirely. Ultimately, however, only one musical number was cut from the film. There was to be a high-energy song called "La La Land," which would have represented the high point in Seb and Mia's romance after Mia decides to quit her job and focus on her one-woman show and Seb decides to take the job with Keith. They would have come together, excited about the plans they had in store, with a triumphant "love will conquer all" approach to their relationship, even while these events would, in hindsight, become the source of their unraveling as a couple.[68] Hurwitz describes how the studio executives loved the song and thought it would become the film's hit number, which in turn gave him and Chazelle pause, as they were resistant to including any song that was too unabashedly upbeat.[69] As pre-production continued, the song seemed to fit less and less with the characters of Mia and Seb, as portrayed by Stone and Gosling. Stone loved the song, but Gosling did not, sensing its more Broadway-inflected pop style. Chazelle recalls that Gosling was the one to suggest reprising "City of Stars" as a duet instead.[70] They were worried about losing a high-energy number at that point in the film, but when the reprise was positioned right before "Start a Fire," the latter became the high-energy song between quieter, more intimate moments. Ultimately, by including a reprise of "City of Stars," they opted for a more naturalistic musical number, rather than the upbeat one that would have been more expected and, in a sense, more predictable. This collaborative decision to cut "La La Land" ended up reinforcing Chazelle's overall aesthetic intent for the film—its realist approach to the musical and the melancholy infused into even the happier moments.

La La Land's Hollywood Narrative

La La Land romanticizes the creative process and the way it informs relationships. Even as it depicts the sacrifices people must make to pursue their art, the film implies that it is possible to pursue an artistically "pure" path without commercial or collaborative sacrifice. Mia finally lands an audition that enables her to "be herself" for a film project that will be built around the actors. Seb ultimately quits the Messengers because of his distaste for their bending to more "popular" commercial considerations, and he is able to build a career for himself as a jazz club owner, which is a "purer" manifestation of his artistic vision. With *La La Land*, it is impossible to ignore the parallels between life and art, between the film's development and production and the narrative it depicts. The process of creating *La La Land* was clearly a feat of talented and persistent individuals pursuing their dreams at all costs, even in the face of setbacks. Indeed, considering the various hurdles that come with producing a blockbuster movie in Hollywood, it is remarkable that Chazelle and Hurwitz were given the chance to make a $30 million film, at a time when Chazelle was still building his reputation and Hurwitz had few compositional credits to his name. It reveals the aesthetic constants between the duo's early projects (particularly the experiments in *Guy and Madeline*) and their higher-profile, higher-budget work.

Of course, as is the case with most Hollywood narratives, the reality was more complex. The film was a collaborative process, a give-and-take between the director and composer and the actors, lyricists, choreographer, and producers. It is the result of a number of creative voices coming together with different perspectives and priorities. Examining the evolution of the film's story and the decisions made during production also reveals the power dynamics and commercial considerations at play, considerations that drive all Hollywood productions. Moreover, it is worth noting that though Chazelle and Hurwitz were inexperienced in the industry, they came from a position of privilege as white, male, Harvard-educated individuals who were quickly able to make important connections in the industry. It is difficult to imagine the same pathway to success with women or writers of color at the helm. The details of *La La Land*'s development lend credence to the film's narrative of pursuing one's dream against all odds, while also pointing to the ways in which it portrays a Hollywood fiction, a story that has been a common Hollywood narrative since the first film musicals.

2

Nostalgia, Homage, and Bittersweet Endings

La La Land and the Classic Film Musical

Ryan Gosling swings around a lamppost in a gesture that strikingly resembles Gene Kelly in *Singin' in the Rain* (1952). Emma Stone sings and dances with her roommates, playing dress-up and joking around just like Maria and her friends in *West Side Story*'s "I Feel Pretty" (1961). Gosling and Stone feign disinterest in each other, only to betray their actual interest by dancing together, much like Fred Astaire and Ginger Rogers's 1930s duets "A Fine Romance" from *Swing Time* (1936) or "Let's Call the Whole Thing Off" from *Shall We Dance* (1937). *La La Land* is packed with these kinds of intertextual references to classic film musicals in its music, narrative, sets, costumes, and cinematography. These classic Hollywood references, deliberately juxtaposed with *La La Land*'s contemporary setting and story, are a crucial aspect of the film's style.

La La Land's references serve multifold purposes. They place the film very clearly and self-consciously in a lineage, drawing a direct connection to itself from the Hollywood musical's Golden Age; as Desirée Garcia suggests, through these references, the film "self-consciously states its own genealogy."[1] They provide some of the film's most joyous moments, offering audiences a chance to revel in one of Hollywood's most cheerful and celebratory genres, disappear temporarily into the escapist pleasures of onscreen singing and dancing, and delight in moments of recognition or discovery. At the same time, they evoke nostalgia for a past time, a nostalgia that is central to the cinematic mythmaking at play in *La La Land*. Importantly, the joy and nostalgia derived from these references are—subtly but intentionally—often undercut by Chazelle and Hurwitz, bringing a degree of cynicism to the film that frequently works in tension with the film's nostalgic impulses.

Nostalgia, defined by media scholar Svetlana Boym as "a sentiment of loss and displacement, but . . . also a romance with one's own fantasy,"[2] drives

La La Land. Hannah Lewis, Oxford University Press. © Oxford University Press 2024.
DOI: 10.1093/9780197682616.003.0003

the motivations of the lead characters. Yet the film's narrative also exhibits ambivalence about the characters' nostalgia. As Anthony Carew claims, the film suggests that being in love with old-fashioned art forms can become a "kind of blinkered nostalgia."[3] Seb and Mia only find success at the expense of their relationship, suggesting that old-fashioned Hollywood endings are incompatible with contemporary life's challenges. The narrative itself therefore sends ambivalent messages about nostalgia, destabilizing the film's own nostalgic aesthetic. Though *La La Land* is in many ways a joyful film, this ambivalence produces a story that has resonated with audiences as feeling uniquely contemporary.

This chapter delves into the various ways that *La La Land* references film musicals of the Golden Age, both through intertextuality—specific references to earlier films—and through reliance on well-known conventions of the film musical genre in its overarching structure and narrative. The cinematic allusions, some extended and some more fleeting, are too numerous to include an exhaustive list here; I focus on some of the most notable sources of homage in the film, particularly the Gene Kelly–Stanley Donen films made for MGM; the Fred Astaire–Ginger Rogers films of the 1930s; and the films of French director Jacques Demy, who himself was intertextually referencing Hollywood musicals in his own films. Throughout, I describe the ways that Chazelle, Hurwitz, and the rest of the creative team simultaneously sought to infuse the film with opposing impulses, a melancholy with a cynical edge. To that end, this chapter also explores the film's tension between nostalgia, homage, and modernity in its music, lyrics, and audiovisual style.

Nostalgia, Intertextuality, and the Film Musical

Nostalgia has been a feature of film musicals since the beginning of the genre.[4] Developing out of the stage musical following the introduction of synchronized sound technology, the Hollywood musical of the 1930s routinely referenced older theatrical forms like vaudeville and minstrelsy. Musical films sentimentally evoked stage genres while engaging in modern cinematic technologies; as audiences became habituated to the technological cutting edge, nostalgia connected them to the familiar elements of human performance in live genres. Golden Age film musicals often used show-within-a-show tropes and other techniques associated with Broadway. As a frequently reflexive genre, the film musical also often referenced Hollywood itself, self-consciously dialoguing with the genre's past in its own medium, which became another means of connecting the past and the present through nostalgia.[5]

Intertextuality, the intentional referencing of one text within another through quotation, allusion, pastiche, parody, or other techniques, is also a familiar phenomenon in both musical theater and film. Often connected to the concept of postmodernism, which is characterized by self-referentiality and recycling of past styles and themes, intertextuality brings layers of meaning into a work, allowing audiences to engage in novel ways with both the new work and the one being referenced. Much like sampling in hip-hop, intertextual plays and films openly celebrate their influences; part of the enjoyment of the genre stems from the pleasure that comes from recognition. At the same time, one need not have familiarity with the specific references to derive joy from an intertextual work. Audiences can engage with the work on a variety of levels of understanding.

On the stage, musical theater is, according to Adam Rush, an "inherently intertextual art form," "continually recycl[ing] other texts and forms."[6] This process has been particularly notable in the 21st century, when many of the highest-profile Broadway shows have recycled source material from popular culture in some form. Whether the show is an adaptation of another well-known film or story (Broadway adaptations of animated Disney films, for instance) or a jukebox musical that features famous pre-existing music (such as *Mamma Mia!*), familiar cultural texts are seen as more certain financial successes. Many "original" shows also participate in this kind of cultural recycling: shows like *Urinetown* (2001), *Avenue Q* (2003), *The Book of Mormon* (2011), and *Hamilton* (2015) make explicit references to musicals from the Broadway canon. Structurally, too, many popular Broadway shows of the 21st century use traditional models established by classic predecessors like Rodgers and Hammerstein, albeit often with a level of detached irony or critical distance.[7] Rush suggests that intertextuality in contemporary musical theater is a "calculated reflection of a culture which is accustomed to seeing familiar texts repackaged and repurposed for a wider audience."[8] In the case of musical theater, intertextual references to popular culture can also serve to expand a show's potential audience by inviting new audiences in.

Intertextuality has also been pervasive in cinematic history, becoming increasingly common in the last decade of the 20th century.[9] Filmmakers like Martin Scorsese, Quentin Tarantino, and the Coen brothers are perhaps some of the best-known examples of late 20th- and early 21st-century auteur filmmakers known for their explicit, self-conscious references to earlier films. In the tradition of New Wave directors like Jean-Luc Godard, Scorsese sees his approach to homage as one he shares with other "film maker cinephiles," who make allusions to characters or narratives, reconstruct shots, or even borrow musical material to communicate their love of specific films or filmmakers.[10] The Coen brothers, on the other hand, "deliberately allude to, imitate, and parody" films to cause a "shock of recognition."[11] Tarantino's approach to homage in such films as *Reservoir Dogs* (1992) and *Pulp Fiction* (1994) has perhaps prompted the most polarized reception: critics disagree about whether Tarantino is "a new and original American talent, a creator-*auteur* close to the real matter of life," or "a film geek-*metteur-en-scène*, a rip-off artist steeped in trash culture and second-hand material."[12] As these three examples can attest, intertextuality has been approached in a number of ways in contemporary cinema, prompting a range of emotional and critical responses. Intertextual references have also become increasingly common in mainstream contemporary cinema, a familiar and almost expected experience for film audiences in an age of frequent remakes, reboots, and franchise spin-offs, of which the Marvel Cinematic Universe is perhaps the most expansive.[13]

It is clear from these examples that intertextuality, homage, and nostalgia are part of the cultural zeitgeist of the first quarter of the 21st century, manifested on both stage and screen. *La La Land* is part of this broader trend, but what perhaps distinguishes it from other contemporary examples is the particular styles and films it is referencing—primarily the mid-century Hollywood musical. As evidenced by the countless articles and online videos pointing out many of the film's references,[14] for audiences already steeped in the film musical genre's history, discovering these "Easter eggs" can prompt joy and a feeling of being "in the know." At the same time, those who are less familiar with the history of the film musical are offered a point of entry into the genre: the references act as a primer for understanding the Hollywood musical's audiovisual and narrative codes, and by extension for better understanding *La La Land* as part of a particular genre history. The other distinctive characteristic of *La La Land*'s intertextuality is the intentional juxtaposition of the nostalgic homage with a contemporary pessimism, manifested in the main characters' disappointments and the fact that their relationship does not work out. The following sections examine the source material that *La La Land* draws from and explore how it is incorporated (and sometimes subverted), first delving into broader generic debts and then turning to more specific references and sources of influence.

Generic Debts and References to "Classic" Hollywood

Chazelle has long been interested in experimenting with juxtapositions of classic Hollywood musical references with modern settings. *Guy and Madeline* set the stage for his approach in *La La Land*, though he claims that he was not consciously thinking about it at first:

> It would be this weird thing where . . . [someone would watch *Guy and Madeline* and be] thrown when they saw a cell phone or something. Because I started to realize, "Wow, I've so inhaled these references that are all from a different era that it just winds up having the effect that everything feels like a period film, or like an artifact from a different era." And I kind of liked that. I liked that there would be these moments of discombobulation here.
>
> The difference with *La La Land* is that we . . . played with it more consciously. We'd be like, "Okay, let's literally have a musical number that is the most old-fashioned Fred Astaire type number in the movie, let's have it be interrupted by a cell phone." Or "Let's have some beautiful [set that] looks like a backlot street with old lamps and everything, but the cars are all Priuses" or something. So . . . we were able to think about it consciously a little bit more.[15]

This juxtaposition of two distinct time periods in filmmaking (broadly characterized as "present" and "past") can create an intentionally jarring effect. Films like *Casablanca* (1942), *Singin' in the Rain,* and *Rebel Without a Cause* (1955) (all referenced in *La La Land*) belong to an era of filmmaking that is colloquially called the "Golden Age," or "classic Hollywood." Using the term "Golden Age," as critics and fans tend to do, automatically buys into a nostalgia for a "better" era of filmmaking, while calling these films "classic" implies that they have a certain timelessness, or even a sense of being out of time.[16] Therefore, *La La Land*'s incorporation of specific references and broader generic markers from the particular time and place depicted in the mid-century Hollywood musical evokes a nostalgia for this older cinematic era and mythologizes it as timeless. This brings modern aspects of the story—cell phones, modern cars, etc.—into sharp relief. Many of the generic markers referenced have become enshrined enough in popular culture to be implicitly recognized as denoting "classic" film, whether or not audience members consciously pick up on them. That *La La Land* employs these markers immediately places it alongside these "classics," simultaneously within and outside of its own time.

The film's music functions in a similar way. According to Chazelle, "There was never really a question of what the style of the music was going to be"—he and Hurwitz wanted it to feel "timeless" or "classic," much in the way the Great American Songbook has become canonized as "classic."[17] According to Chazelle, they did not want the music to ground the story in a specific time or place; instead, they decided "to work within this vernacular that is based on things that have lasted for longer than the past twenty years. They've stood the test of time a little bit more.... We were borrowing a lot from the Beach Boys; we were borrowing a lot from the Beatles. Obviously borrowing a ton from jazz and a ton from French stuff. So it was going to be this kind of mix."[18] Just like the "classic" of classic Hollywood cinema, the impulse behind the musical style was to create something "timeless." However, while many of the songs that comprise the Great American Songbook come from Tin Pan Alley, Broadway, and Hollywood of the early to mid-20th century—including films that are visually referenced in *La La Land*—Hurwitz's music for *La La Land* is more indebted to mid-century musicals, jazz, and 1960s pop, than to the likes of Harold Arlen, Irving Berlin, Jerome Kern, and George Gershwin. Nevertheless, the songs in *La La Land* are intended to evoke a different time and place, one that feels "classic" and "timeless," particularly when contrasted with other popular musical styles in the film (such as the 1980s synth pop of Seb's cover band or the jazz-inflected R&B of the Messengers).

A 21st-Century Couple in a Mid-Century Musical Film

La La Land is shaped by the classic Hollywood musical in ways both broad and specific. Its generic debts can be seen most clearly through its narrative structure and reflexive impulses, which help deliver the contemporary story and setting through a decidedly vintage lens.

The Dual-Focus Narrative

One of the features of *La La Land*'s plot is its dual-focus narrative, which Rick Altman identifies as one of the primary things that distinguishes the film musical genre from other cinematic genres:

> Instead of focusing all its interest on a single central character, following the trajectory of her progress, the American film musical . . . [is] built around parallel stars of opposite sex and radically divergent values. This dual-focus structure requires the viewer to be sensitive not so much to chronology and progression—for the outcome of the male/female match is entirely conventional and thus quite predictable—but to simultaneity and comparison.[19]

According to Altman, with a dual-focus narrative, cause-and-effect is less important than parallelisms, and the plot "depends not on the stars' falling in love . . . but on the resolution of their differences. Each must adopt the characteristics of the other."[20] Film musicals demonstrate this duality through a series of paired segments matching the male and female leads. Often, the basic sexual duality of the leading couple is paired with a second duality: "One side of the thematic dichotomy is closely associated with the work ethic and its values, while the other is devoted to those activities and qualities traditionally identified with entertainment."[21] The working out and resolution of this secondary dichotomy—the assimilation of hard work and entertainment into one—as its thematic center serves as implicit justification for the film musical genre itself, as the quintessential example of entertainment.

La La Land, at least initially, perfectly embodies this duality that is a common, almost expected feature of the classic Hollywood film musical. The audience first meets Mia and Seb from their cars in a Los Angeles traffic jam, which is also the couple's first encounter. We first see Seb in his 1982 Buick Riviera convertible, listening to a Thelonious Monk recording on his tape player, rewinding and replaying the same section over and over again. The camera travels to Mia's Toyota Prius, where she appears to be having a trite conversation on her phone about a drunk friend. But then she stops, lowers her phone from her ear, and looks at a piece of paper—it turns out that Mia is rehearsing her lines for an audition. She does not notice that the cars in front of her have begun to move, and Seb leans on his horn and abruptly changes lanes to pass her. She gives him the finger, then drives away. This opening scene establishes Seb as someone with a clear preference for things of the past—through his vintage car and his classic bebop cassette tape—and Mia as someone clearly trying her hardest to succeed in the present.

As the film progresses, we are first given a glimpse into Mia's life and her struggles: her unfulfilling job at the coffee shop on the Warner Bros. studio lot, her clear acting talent at the audition that is ignored by casting directors as she finds herself amidst a sea of actresses that look like her, her demoralization but ultimate resolve as she decides to join her roommates at a party, and her self-doubt as she looks at herself in the bathroom mirror. After leaving the party, she walks by a restaurant and hears piano music that captivates her (Seb playing "Mia & Sebastian's Theme"). The moment seems to transport her, briefly suggesting that there might be something more for her in life. But as the camera slowly zooms on her face, with the rest of the scene in black, a single sustained note suddenly becomes louder, taking over the music and transforming into Seb's car horn from earlier that day.

The scene then cuts back to the moment of their heated interaction earlier that day, this time following Seb. In Seb's first scenes, we are introduced to a character stuck in an older time—one that he is too young to have experienced first-hand—and frustrated with the rest of the world for refusing to acknowledge the greatness of these things past (his distaste for the historic Van Beek jazz club being turned into a "samba-tapas club," his sister carelessly sitting on Hoagy Carmichael's stool, his boss at the restaurant requiring him to play cheesy Christmas songs rather than allowing him to play jazz). He ultimately strays from the restaurant owner's prescribed setlist, which leads him to lose his job. This is the moment when Mia overhears his playing. She tries to talk to him, but he brusquely pushes her aside, leaving in a huff.

Mia and Seb continue to be portrayed as embodying different values in their next interaction, where Seb is playing in an '80s cover band at a party. Mia mocks Seb when he claims to be "a serious musician" while dressed in ridiculous '80s clothing (an echo of Kathy Seldon's claim to be a "serious actress" in *Singin' in the Rain* before she jumps out of a cake as a chorus girl), and Seb, in turn, makes fun of her calling herself an actress when she has yet to land a role. Only after the party, when the two are walking to their cars, is there a hint of their compatibility, symbolized by their singing and dancing together in "A Lovely Night."

As the couple finally comes together, we see each beginning to adopt some of the values of the other. Over the course of the film, Seb begins to acknowledge his need to make the music he so idolizes accessible to others. And Mia, in turn, learns she must be true to her own artistic voice—a voice that resembles a classic Hollywood movie star more than a contemporary one—in order to find success as an actor. They each end up tipping the scales too far in the other direction: Seb "sells out" through his work with the Messengers, and Mia quits her job to focus on her one-woman play, causing conflict and tension in their relationship. They ultimately realize they are each embracing the other's view of success, and they both take steps to be more authentic to their own artistic voice. Though not a traditional merging of work ethics and entertainment, it is a contemporary variation on the same theme: the assimilation of adaptation and artistic integrity. Their conflict in the middle of the film intensifies when their definitions of "success" diverge. Even though the couple does not end up together, their respective successes—Seb as a jazz club owner, and Mia as a famous actress—are shown to be a genuine reflection of the assimilation of each one's values.

A Modern Relationship

At the same time, the couple's relationship is depicted as fundamentally different from those seen in most earlier film musicals. Mia and Seb are dreamers confronting very modern problems. They must struggle to make a living in Los Angeles, a city that seems to keep beating them down. As Seb says of Angelenos, "They worship everything and they value nothing." Of course, many characters in earlier films have struggled to make it in L.A., with varying degrees of success. But as critic Diana Dabrowska suggests, "the conceit of California as a place where a person cannot distinguish between winter and spring becomes a suggestive background for a generation that seems lost en route to true self-determination—there is no map showing the way from 'La La Land' to the real Los Angeles. The characters are stuck in their dreams, like rebels without a cause."[22] Ultimately, although Mia and Seb are dreamers, they have to confront varying realities that butt up against their ambitions of success. For Seb, it is trying to determine the degree to which he is willing to compromise his aesthetic values in exchange for success. For Mia, it is trying to figure out when to "give up," when the industry has beat her down too many times for her to stand back up and try again. Seb and Mia ultimately sacrifice their relationship to pursue their individual dreams, a poignant ending that denies audiences the old-fashioned love story expected in earlier musicals and suggests that these kinds of happy endings cannot be fully realized in today's world. According to Steven Cohan, the film is built on "a tension between the utopian spirit of musicals and a dystopian sense of the ordinary world," the latter of which is embodied in the leading couple's professional and personal struggles.[23]

Reflexivity

Film musical scholars like Rick Altman and Jane Feuer have argued that the Hollywood musical is an inherently self-referential genre. The common subgenre of the Hollywood musical, called the "show musical" or backstage musical—one whose plot is centered on putting on a show—is inherently reflexive. Altman suggests that "the show musical gives us the illusion of seeing something which theatergoers cannot perceive"[24] while symbolically creating a community onscreen. The creation of a show is often paralleled with the formation of a romantic couple, whose success in their relationship symbolically hinges on the success of the performance.[25] The backstage musical subgenre was particularly prevalent in the early sound era, with films like *The Broadway Melody* (1929), *42nd Street* (1933), and *Gold Diggers of 1933* (1933) giving diegetic justification for musical performances. It again became widespread during the heyday of the MGM Freed Unit, with *Babes in Arms* (1939), *The Barkleys of Broadway* (1949), *Singin' in the Rain* (1952), *The Band Wagon* (1953), and others.

According to Jane Feuer, the "self-reflective musical" served to affirm the film musical's own values for a popular audience, contrasting successful entertainment with performances that fail to please audiences, thereby "mythifying" entertainment.[26] In self-reflective (or reflexive) musicals, performances that don't take place onstage often appear to be a "spontaneous outpouring of emotion."[27] Techniques like bricolage, where characters extemporaneously perform with whatever props may be at hand, seem to naturalize performances, "lend[ing] an irresistible aura of spontaneity to numbers which in reality are feats of technological know-how."[28] *Singin' in the Rain* is perhaps the best-known example, purporting to draw back the curtain on what goes into filmmaking itself.

La La Land is a reflexive musical, and it even fits some of the qualities of a backstage musical or "show musical." It takes place in Hollywood, focuses on a musician and an actress, and follows their trials and tribulations as they try to make it in the entertainment industry. Simply put, it is a movie musical about music and the movies. Both leads perform diegetically and nondiegetically during the film, like in most backstage musicals. The film features moments of bricolage, from Mia and her roommates' mimicking an Oscars acceptance speech with a tissue box in "Someone in the Crowd" to Sebastian's borrowing a hat from a passerby and flipping it in his hand in "City of Stars." Mia has a giant picture of Ingrid Bergman on her wall, an imposing visual reminder of her own desire to be a movie star. And the couple finally begins to connect and to stop denying their interest in each other when they take a stroll on a studio lot, where they see up close the artificiality that goes into making a film. This scene is strikingly similar to a corresponding one in *Singin' in the Rain* when Kathy and Don begin to fall in love as they walk through the studio.[29] And the countless overt references to specific films from Hollywood history is another reflexive move, heightening the spectator's awareness of the film's status as a musical and self-consciously placing *La La Land* within a lineage of beloved musical films.

Homage Once Removed: The Influence of Jacques Demy

While the references to mid-century Hollywood are likely the most recognizable for American audiences, *La La Land* is perhaps most indebted to the film musicals of French director Jacques Demy. Understanding the significance of Demy's films—and of French filmmaking more generally—on Chazelle and Hurwitz's style reveals their engagement with the classic Hollywood musical to be more intertextually layered than initially meets the eye. Demy's musical films *Les Parapluies de Cherbourg* (1964) and *Les Demoiselles de Rochefort* (1967) combined homage to classic Hollywood musicals with French New Wave sensibilities. His take on the film musical was singular, steeped in French cultural and cinematic traditions, while also very clearly indebted to the Hollywood films he sought to emulate. Therefore, one of Chazelle and Hurwitz's biggest sources of inspiration came from a director who, in many ways, had already done fifty years earlier what they sought to do: appropriate, reinterpret, and subvert classic Hollywood musical references. Demy took on the Hollywood musical but gave it a decidedly French twist, something Chazelle, very influenced by French cinema himself, was eager to emulate.

As recounted in Chapter 1, Chazelle has frequently and publicly declared *Les Parapluies de Cherbourg* to be his favorite film musical and his "gateway drug" into the genre. He claims it was the first musical he had seen that "mirrors life":

> It's not just that it doesn't end happily, because I'd seen *West Side Story* . . .
> but [*West Side Story*] is operatic and grand tragedy. . . . Whereas *Umbrellas
> of Cherbourg*, I really found myself thrown for a loop when they have this
> reunion non-reunion at the end and just go their separate ways. . . . I didn't
> know you could do that in a musical. So what else could you do in a musical
> that I haven't thought about?
>
>   . . . The fact that the [film's] artificiality proved not just *not* a hindrance,
> but maybe even a kind of additive to the emotion, I think, fascinated me
> and probably prompted me to re-watch it over and over again during those
> early years, and try to decipher how it pulled off this kind of magic trick.[30]

Demy was a specific point of influence, of course, but Chazelle was also
drawn to what he considered a more general French cinematic sensibility
that he aimed to emulate in his films: an "interplay" of tonal extremes, of
happy and sad:

> You see it in [Jean] Renoir, you could even argue you see it in French
> painting. . . . And we have names for it, you might refer to it as poetic realism,
> or romantic fatalism. . . . There are different names for different iterations of
> it throughout French history. But the consistent thing is just this idea that
> . . . you can have a candy-colored musical and the lovers don't wind up to-
> gether. Or that you can have, on the flip side, a movie about people living in
> slums, like a Renoir movie [such as his 1936 film *Les Bas-fonds*], beggars on
> the street, dying of this or that, but they've got a great baguette and a bottle
> of wine.
>
>   So, for *La La Land*, it was just, again, one of these formulations, of just
> "let's never let any song or melody, and by the same token, lyric, ever be
> completely one thing or the other."[31]

For Chazelle, Demy's blend of light poeticism and deeper poignancy, even
tragedy, was a quality that placed his films in a distinctly French lineage, and
this was an aspect of French cinema that he sought to capture in *La La Land*.

Les Parapluies de Cherbourg and *Les Demoiselles de Rochefort* are different
in many ways: *Cherbourg* is sung-through, while *Rochefort* has distinct musical numbers. *Cherbourg* more explicitly tackles social issues in postwar
France like the toll of the war in Algeria, premarital sex, and economic hardship, in contrast to *Rochefort*'s generally lighter tone; *Cherbourg*'s ending is not
happy, whereas *Rochefort* (just barely) ends happily, with each pair of lovers

being united in the end. But they both share a rich, saturated color palette; a larger-than-life depiction of the mundane; a distinctive approach to camerawork; a lushly orchestrated, jazz-inflected score by Michel Legrand; and a blend of melancholy and ebullience. *Cherbourg* hints at its Hollywood musical influences obliquely, through its musical and visual style, only to thwart those expectations in its unusual musical mode of delivery. *Rochefort* is more explicit in its references, with even casting decisions—in particular Gene Kelly and George Chakiris (who was Bernardo in *West Side Story*)—evoking Hollywood musicals. There are playfully reflexive moments that point both to Demy's debt to American cinema and to his films' distinctiveness. For instance, in *Rochefort*, characters sing about the music of Duke Ellington, Louis Armstrong, and Count Basie, only for another character to say they prefer Legrand's music. Perhaps most significantly, both films deal with loss, missed connections, and unfulfilled desires. And each one represents fantasy and reality onscreen simultaneously, often blurring the boundaries between the two. These are all stylistic elements found in *La La Land*.

One of the most obvious points of connection between *Les Parapluies de Cherbourg* and *La La Land* is the fact that the protagonists are not together at the end. This is not without precedent in Hollywood: films as early as *The Smiling Lieutenant* (1931) thwarted the expectation that the couple end up together, and some film musicals, like *A Star is Born* (1954), have a tragic ending.[32] But *La La Land* and *Cherbourg* share a bittersweetness, a story where factors both internal and external to the romance lead each member of the couple in different directions. Both films' endings poignantly suggest what might have been, had the couple remained together, before they again go their separate ways. The blend of disillusionment with bright, optimistic color palettes and audiovisual spectacle pervades both Demy's musicals and *La La Land*.

There are many specific visual references to Demy's films as well, from the opening choreography of "Another Day of Sun" resembling the opening of *Les Demoiselles de Rochefort*, to the brief shot of an umbrella shop on the studio set. Chazelle's distinctive camerawork, particularly his winding long takes, resembles many of Demy's shots, such as the one in *Rochefort*, right after the opening credits, where the camera travels in a single, unbroken shot into the window of an apartment above the city square. Additionally, both *Cherbourg* and *La La Land* are structured into chapters that are signaled visually with title screens ("Departure," "Absence," and "Return" in *Cherbourg*, and named after the four seasons in *La La Land*).

Hurwitz was also clearly influenced by Legrand's scores to Demy's films. He mentions that the elements that stuck out to him about Legrand's music for these two films were his use of "sequences and circles . . . and the way that lush orchestra was married to a jazz rhythm section."[33] Legrand's influence permeates each number in *La La Land* differently, but a recurring similarity is Hurwitz's incorporation of circles of fifths. In Legrand's well-known "Chanson des Jumelles" from *Les Demoiselles de Rochefort* (Musical Example 2.1a), for instance, the circle of fifths is one of the most audibly striking aspects of the song, structuring the chorus and creating a sense of harmonic unity. The vocal line is built around a short melodic motive that is transposed several times as the chords move through the sequence, which bolsters the melody and makes it especially memorable. In *La La Land*, we can hear a similar harmonic-melodic interplay in the song "A Lovely Night" (Musical Example 2.1b).

As enumerated above, *La La Land*'s many Hollywood references are filtered in numerous ways through Chazelle and Hurwitz's emulation of the Demy-Legrand films. For many American audiences, these references are easier to miss, or mistaken for more straightforward Hollywood references. Still, even if Chazelle and Hurwitz borrowed heavily from the Demy-Legrand films, these stylistic elements have a different effect when seen in a contemporary Hollywood film than in a French film from the 1960s. This borrowing thus creates an interesting circularity: *La La Land* includes earlier Hollywood generic references, depicted through the lens of a French cinematic sensibility and subversion of these very references, to create an updated take on that genre within contemporary Hollywood. Rather than being purely emulation, it is homage, once removed.

A Blend of References: "Another Day of Sun" and "Someone in the Crowd"

Of course, *La La Land* also contains numerous direct, straightforward audiovisual references to specific Hollywood films. These references comprise some of the more joyful moments of the film: the joy stems both from the recognition of specific references and from the pleasure of seeing them transposed into an unexpected context. Both "Another Day of Sun" and "Someone in the Crowd," the film's two big ensemble numbers in the first fifteen minutes, are chock full of references both overt and less so, prompting

Musical Example 2.1a Michel Legrand, "Chanson des Jumelles" (excerpt), *Les Demoiselles de Rochefort* (1967) (my transcription)

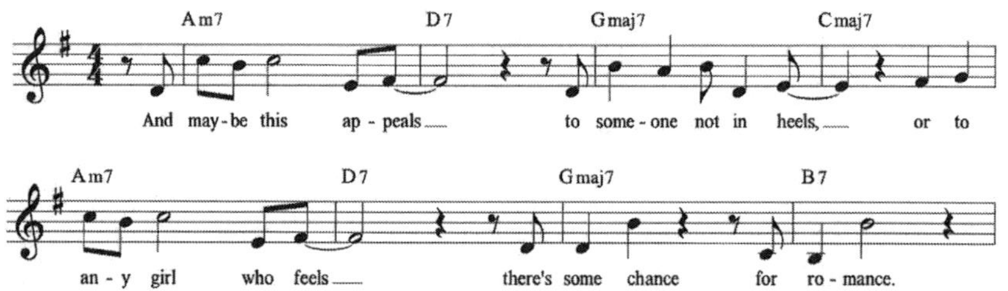

Musical Example 2.1b Justin Hurwitz, "A Lovely Night" (excerpt), *La La Land* (2016)

exciting moments of recognition for film musical fans. At the same time, the ebullience of these two numbers is tempered by an underlying hesitance, even cynicism.

"Another Day of Sun" fulfills many of the functions of a classic opening number: it establishes setting, community, and a world where characters express themselves through song. Critic A. O. Scott suggests that the number "is the movie's way of auditioning for the audience, testing our tolerance for a bold blend of nostalgia and novelty. Can a generation raised on *Glee* and the *High School Musical* franchise and besotted by newfangled stage musicals like *Book of Mormon* and *Hamilton* find room in its heart for a movie that unabashedly evokes *The Young Girls of Rochefort* and *An American in Paris?*"[34] It blends nostalgia and novelty through its engagement with the styles and conventions of earlier films, while adapting them to a contemporary setting.

The number opens with the sound of car horns blaring. A brief snippet of Tchaikovsky's *1812 Overture* plays before we hear a radio dial tuning to a different station, where an announcer declares another hot sunny day in Southern California. A cacophony of car horns and radios follows, as the camera slowly pans down from the sunny sky to cars stuck in a traffic jam. We hear different music from car radios as the camera pans to each car, including classical music, rock, hip-hop, and even a brief snippet of "It Happened at Dawn," a song from Chazelle's earlier film *Guy and Madeline*. From this discord emerges the opening piano riff of "Another Day of Sun," and the other sounds begin to fade away as the camera fixes on the first singer. Chazelle claims that the "germ of the idea" for the opening came from his misremembering of a shot he believed came from *Taxi Driver* (1976)— which, he later realized, was actually the opening scene from *Touch of Evil* (1958)—where the camera travels from car to car, the sound traveling along with the camera. He thought it "would be cool to do a kind of sonic tapestry like that, with each person in their own bubble of their car, [which] lends itself really well to L.A., and the experience of gridlock in L.A. And it seemed to lend itself to this idea of how . . . nondiegetic music can emerge from diegetic music and set the tone."[35]

Regardless of the specific source of inspiration, the opening contains many similarities to the opening of the 1932 musical *Love Me Tonight*, which depicts a Parisian city street waking up through a "Symphony of Noises," a rhythmic repetition of gestures that creates layers of repeated sounds. In *Love Me Tonight*, the Parisian setting is introduced sonically: the music of the opening number first seems to come diegetically from a woman's phonograph, and the orchestra and sounds of the street mix together until the sound effects eventually fade out and Maurice Chevalier, the film's lead, sings an opening song. "Another Day of Sun" also, by Chazelle's own admission, draws stylistically on the opening of *Les Demoiselles de Rochefort*. According to choreographer Mandy Moore, Chazelle "liked the idea of starting out with very little dance. He referenced the beginning of *The Young Girls of Rochefort*—he loved that people were getting out of this truck and

(a)

(b)

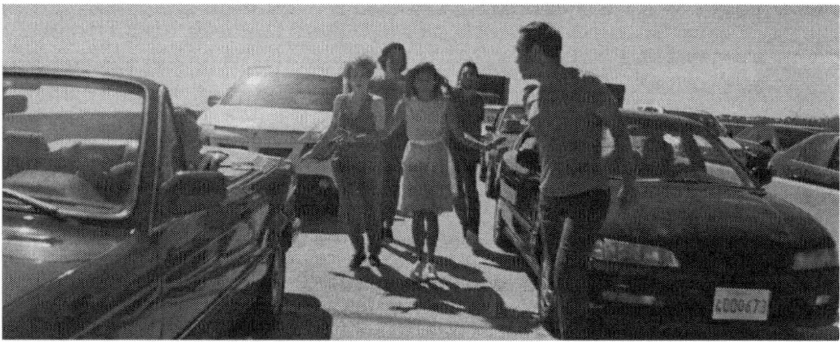

Figures 2.1a–b Opening, *Les Demoiselles de Rochefort* (1967), and "Another Day of Sun," *La La Land* (2016)

starting to stretch and yawn, so that was the reference for the beginning of the number."[36] Indeed, in both numbers, the characters emerge from their vehicles and begin with natural gestures that slowly become increasingly stylized until they morph into full-blown choreography (Figures 2.1a–b). Chazelle also mentions influences from *West Side Story*'s "Prologue," where an entire physical setting is introduced primarily through choreography, and *The Lion King*, where the film's title comes right at the end of the opening number.[37]

The song opens with bright, full orchestration, punctuated by brass stings. The nameless characters sing—first individually, then together—about the draw of Los Angeles and the dream of making it big, a theme found in countless Hollywood movies about Hollywood. Other audiovisual aspects of the song place it in an older cinematic world. The cars seen in the beginning of the scene are somewhat older, more difficult to anchor in a specific time and place. The costumes are bright, solid colors that recall costuming in early Technicolor musicals. The song also embodies the "aesthetic of spontaneity" found in so many Hollywood musicals, with the highway becoming an impromptu site of song and dance. At the same time, certain elements place it firmly in the present day: the racial diversity of the ensemble, which was rarely, if ever, a feature of mid-century film musicals; the crisp, contemporary vocal performance styles; and the band that emerges from the truck in the middle of the scene.

Amidst the upbeat music and performance style, there is a strain of pessimism prevalent in the music and lyrics that temper the unabashed enthusiasm of the scene. This tension between nostalgia and cynicism is embodied in the music and lyrics of many of the songs. In my conversation with Benj Pasek and Justin Paul, Paul discussed the balance they attempted to strike in the lyrics:

> The thing that we were always pursuing was the balance of realism, and that we were telling a contemporary story, and yet there *was* a certain heightened sense to it, and there *was* a theatricality to the filmmaking. While we wanted to make it feel grounded in real stakes and make the characters feel real and not as broadly drawn as a classic movie musical, Damien was still very much capturing the magic and romanticism of some of the classic movie musicals. So, I think each song we were kind of approaching—some songs more than others, I think—but, in sum, we were approaching them, writing them, trying to keep these two things hand in hand: one, of writing something that feels contemporary and relevant enough, and yet knowing that we were writing in a style that at least could certainly facilitate a more heightened style of filmmaking. . . . So, if anything, I'd say we were always trying to straddle the line between something that felt relevant and realist and yet could hold something that was more a flight of fancy. . . .
>
> I think that's the lovely thing about setting a romantic musical in the era now, and telling a contemporary story. There's going to inevitably be something that seems complicated about it, and therefore melancholy. And yet, by its very identity and definition, making something musical means making something aspirational. And especially about L.A. In a city of dreamers and people with hopes and wishes and dreams, and a musical, all those things hand in hand do make it so aspirational, and yet, there is some bitter with the sweet.[38]

This balance of ebullience and melancholy is apparent even in the most energetic ensemble numbers, like "Another Day of Sun." The singers recount what they gave up to come to L.A. and pursue their dreams: "And when they let you down/You get up off the ground,/The mornin' rolls around, and it's another day of sun." The song is visually stunning and musically upbeat, but with an underlying cynical or pessimistic strain. As Pasek said, "There's this fantastical [aspect], we're on the highway and we're dancing and all this, but it's about addressing the practical realities of dreaming, but also how difficult it is. That we're striving for something that's really tough."[39] Chazelle succinctly called them "lyrics about failure."[40]

Musically, the song may appear more straightforwardly upbeat. The song opens with a cheerful accompaniment, characterized by a syncopated piano line and brass punctuation. But Chazelle points out that although Hurwitz's "orchestration is super aggressive, and the dancing, everyone's smiling, so you get this [impression of] 'oh, it's super happy' . . . the actual melody, especially of the verse (and you hear this more if someone were to just play it on a piano rubato), it's actually pretty sad. It's pretty minor."[41] Hurwitz, too, acknowledged how "on a music theory level," there are aspects of his compositional style that intentionally blend the cheerful and the melancholy: "I cadence in minor and then I cadence in major, and things like that. . . . That's just more instinct, but I'm aware of it."[42] Moore also described having felt these qualities in the music when choreographing the number:

> It was never this exuberant dance, it always had this grounded heaviness to it for some reason. And I think a lot of it was that music. The notes for that are "da-da-da" [sings the melody "just another day of sun"], it was way up there, but then underneath it was like "da-da-da" [sings the opening instrumental melody]. It had all that rounded base to it. And the idea of these characters, these people that are dreamers, but work a job that doesn't align with their dreams, there is something so beautiful about that, and not just tipping too much to one side of "Everything's butterflies and bunnies," but also "Everything just sucks." You can have both of those ways of thinking and feeling within the same person.[43]

Whether or not it is perceptible to the listener, Hurwitz and Chazelle intended this blend of upbeat enthusiasm and somewhat hidden pessimism to set the tone for the rest of the film, what Chazelle calls an "undercutting" of the "traditional, bombastic musical number from old Hollywood."[44]

"Someone in the Crowd," the other big, upbeat ensemble number, also blends references from a number of earlier films. Here, Mia's roommates try to encourage her to come to a party that night, saying that you never know when you will meet the person who will end up being the connection to your success. They playfully banter back and forth before the roommates leave Mia at home. Mia has a change of heart and joins them. Once at the party, we see (through choreography and pantomime) Mia have several apparently unsatisfying conversations with strangers at the party. She goes into the bathroom and sings to herself in the mirror, expressing her own self-doubts and vulnerability; this introspective section of the song is related to the "I Want" musical number tradition, where protagonists express their hopes for their life near the beginning of a film or show. When Mia reemerges, we see the excitement at the party—a man jumping into a pool, the camera spinning underwater from his point of view, while the partygoers dance around the pool and the song ends in literal fireworks.

Moore described the first part of the number, where Mia playfully interacts with her roommates, as "a combination of friendship, in girls being girls, but also there's a little competition in there because they're all doing the same thing. . . . And a little bit of fun and a little bit of whimsical. I felt like there needed to be a bit of magic in there, too . . . there needed to be play. Without it being childish."[45] The number is structured by the movement of the camera, in a single unbroken shot, through the roommates' apartment. It is also structured visually through its use of bright, primary colors, which are foregrounded in the scene, shot against the solid colors of the apartment walls.

This first part of the song shares many similarities with the staging of "I Feel Pretty" from the 1961 film adaptation of *West Side Story*, which features a space where the women playfully interact. Maria is set apart from the other women in her giddy expression of love, but they ultimately are all rooting for her as they play with the fabric in the sewing shop and dance around the space. The song also references Bob Fosse's *Sweet Charity* (1969), which depicts a group of women friends who all work as dancers-for-hire. In the song "There's Got to Be Something Better Than This," the women determinedly sing about how they want out of their profession. The three dance passionately on the rooftop, in sync with each other, directly facing the camera. When Mia and her roommates leave their apartment to go to the party, their synchronized dance is much more subdued, but it still makes clear references to *Sweet Charity* (Figures 2.2a–b). By combining references

(a)

(b)

Figures 2.2a–b "There's Got to Be Something Better Than This," *Sweet Charity* (1969), and "Someone in the Crowd," *La La Land* (2016)

to the giddy excitement of "I Feel Pretty" and the worldly cynicism of "There's Got to Be Something Better Than This," "Someone in the Crowd" sets the tone of an upbeat, energetic, exciting ensemble number with a touch of dissatisfaction.

There are other, more fleeting references in the number—a brief aerial shot that mimics the kaleidoscopic shapes of Busby Berkeley's chorus girl numbers, a montage of Los Angeles neon lights on their way to the party that resembles a similar montage in *Singin' in the Rain*, and even the pool camera shot from *Boogie Nights*. But the visual spectacle of the end of the scene, jam-packed with references, ultimately feels somewhat vacuous because of Mia's feelings of alienation. Again, like "Another Day of Sun," the song is bright and energetic, but with an air of cynicism in its message.

The Astaire-Rogers Films: "A Lovely Night"

The first song Mia and Seb sing together is "A Lovely Night." Narratively, the song is significant because it is the first moment that explicitly teases their romance to come. They are walking from the party, looking for their cars. Their banter is playful, taking gentle gibes at each other but in an almost flirtatious way. Then they happen upon a beautiful vista of Los Angeles at sunset. They both joke that it's "not much to look at," but they are clearly taken by its beauty. The musical underscoring steadily builds up until it serves as its introduction to their song. Seb swings around a lamppost (a brief nod to Gene Kelly's famous gesture in *Singin' in the Rain*) as he begins to sing about how the setting is romantic but wasted on the two of them: "We've stumbled on a view/that's tailor-made for two/What a shame that two are you and me." He continues about how the two of them could never be, singing that their time together is "a waste of a lovely night." Mia's verse is slightly more acerbic, as she sings about how she could never fall for him, and how she's "frankly feeling nothing" toward him. She sits on a park bench and begins to change from her heels into tap shoes. Seb sits down next to her, as the two of them punctuate their interactions with stylized gestures that slowly turn into more elaborate choreography, in sync with the syncopated horn stings. They eventually get up from the bench and begin dancing in parallel around it, with the sunset in the background. As they finish their dance, they lean in close, clearly feeling something more for each other, only for the magic of the moment to be interrupted by Mia's phone ringing in her bag. The whole number was shot on location in a single take, a challenging feat given that they needed to capture the scene during "magic hour."

This number fits into a category of duets sung between leading couples that occur early in a story: the conditional love song. In songs like *Show Boat*'s "Only Make Believe," *Carousel*'s "If I Loved You," or *Oklahoma!*'s "People Will Say We're in Love," the male and female lead sing together about how they are not in love, only to betray their own feelings for each other, foreshadowing their eventual coupling later in the story. More specifically, "A Lovely Night" is modeled after the songs of this type sung and danced by Fred Astaire and Ginger Rogers in their 1930s RKO films. The Fred and Ginger films frequently featured a song twinged with sarcasm, where they feign disinterest in each other. As soon as they dance together, their true feelings are revealed and it becomes clear how perfect a match they are for each other. Songs like "Pick Yourself Up" from *Swing Time* and "Let's Call the

Whole Thing Off" from *Shall We Dance* fit this formula. In the latter song, the two sit on a bench wearing roller skates, each sing a verse, then begin their choreography sitting on the bench before they stand up and continue dancing, a gesture that "A Lovely Night" clearly borrows.

"Isn't It a Lovely Day (to Be Caught in the Rain)" from *Top Hat* (1935) is perhaps the clearest parallel to "A Lovely Night": even the title bears some similarity. According to Moore, this was one of the numbers that Chazelle suggested she watch for inspiration. She claims that he "loved how at the start of the number they're possibly enemies, and by the end through their dancing, they have learned to be attracted. So basically what I had to do is I had to go from 'I don't like you' to 'Mmm, maybe I like you.'"[46] In "Isn't It a Lovely Day," Astaire and Rogers get caught under a gazebo in a rainstorm. They sit down as Astaire sings to Rogers, and then he stands and begins dancing. For most of the number, the two dance in parallel, together but not touching, another clear stylistic trait that "A Lovely Night" borrows (Figures 2.3a, 2.3c). This kind of parallel choreography is also featured in a later Astaire number from *The Band Wagon*, "Dancing in the Dark," where he partnered with Cyd Charisse (Figure 2.3b). Furthermore, Astaire's dance numbers famously feature long takes, although they are not one-shots like "A Lovely Night." However, in both "Isn't It a Lovely Day" and "Dancing in the Dark," Astaire and his partner ultimately touch, dancing close together with their arms around each other, rather than remaining in parallel. In "A Lovely Night," with a brief exception where Seb takes Mia's hand for her to twirl, the two do not touch, perhaps a subtle hint that this romance will end differently—that despite their compatibility, the two will not wind up together in the end.[47]

"City of Stars": A Melancholy Love Song

The film's melancholy cynicism is perhaps most obviously on display in the Oscar-winning "City of Stars." Sebastian first sings the song after he and Mia spend the day together, walking on the studio lot and going to a jazz club.[48] They have just agreed to meet up a few days later to go see *Rebel Without a Cause* at the Rialto. There is clearly the possibility of a budding romance between the two of them, but they have not yet kissed. The song's sparse piano accompaniment begins, a slow B minor arpeggiation with a flat seven, while we see the two of them at the Lighthouse Cafe. The camera then cuts to the exterior of the cafe as the two say goodbye, then to Seb walking by himself along the pier. The streetlights twinkle and the setting sun has created a

(a)

(b)

(c)

Figures 2.3a–c "Isn't It a Lovely Day," *Top Hat* (1935), "Dancing in the Dark," *The Band Wagon* (1953), and "A Lovely Night," *La La Land* (2016)

beautiful, colorful sky. Seb whistles along to the minor melody as he stares out at the water. He finds a hat lying by a bench and picks it up as he begins to sing: "City of Stars/Are you shining just for me?" He flips the hat in his hand, the camera following him as he slowly walks toward it and sings, "City of Stars/There's so much that I can't see." The camera follows as he hands the hat to a man who just happens to be on the same pier and briefly dances with the woman who is with him. She seems to enjoy the dance, but after her partner gives Seb a look, he steps back and the couple begins to dance together. Throughout this, he sings: "Who knows? Is this the start of something wonderful and new?/Or one more dream that I cannot make true?" The whole scene was shot in a single take, with the camera following Seb and turning around him as he walks along the pier.

In terms of narrative placement and visual style, the number evokes the title song from *Singin' in the Rain*. Just like Don Lockwood sings of his love for Kathy Seldon in "Singin' in the Rain," Seb sings to himself about the romantic feelings he is developing for Mia. Both songs take place in the evening after the couple has just parted ways. Both performers engage with their environment, interacting briefly with other passersby, but mostly singing to themselves. The hat Seb finds even resembles Gene Kelly's hat in the scene, and the streetlamps on the pier bring the famous *Singin' in the Rain* streetlamp back to mind. The irony, of course, in *Singin' in the Rain* is that the weather is in contradiction with Don's feelings: "The sun's in my heart and I'm ready for love." In "City of Stars," the inverse is true: the weather and setting are perfect, as they always are in Los Angeles, but Seb's feelings are uncertain. He is hesitant to get excited about his new potential love interest, for fear that it will not work out.

This hesitance is mirrored in the music and its interplay with the lyrics. The song's minor key and sparse orchestration contrast with "Singin' in the Rain." In the first line, the chords move from B minor to E major, then cadence in F-sharp minor while Seb sings optimistically of the city shining just for him. The melody repeats, but this time, the chord progression ends with A major as he sings of his uncertainty: "There's so much that I can't see" (Musical Example 2.2). In other words, the lyrics and music work against each other: the music offers hesitancy as the lyrics suggest optimism, followed by the reverse. Hurwitz described the musical progression as "the sad cadence to the sweeter cadence" that is "so essential to that song."[49] The song ends as tentatively as it began, with Seb whistling, the accompaniment continuing even as the camera has dissolved to the next scene.

Musical Example 2.2 "City of Stars" (excerpt), *La La Land* (2016)

City Of Stars
from LA LA LAND
Music by Justin Hurwitz
Lyrics by Benj Pasek & Justin Paul
© 2016 Justin Hurwitz Music (BMI), Warner-Tamerlane Publishing Corp. (BMI), administered by
  Warner-Tamerlane Publishing Corp. (BMI), and B Lion Music (BMI) administered by Songs
  Of Universal, Inc. (BMI)/Pick In A Pinch Music (ASCAP), breathelike music (ASCAP), WC
  Music Corp. (ASCAP) administered by WC Music Corp. (ASCAP) and A Lion Music (ASCAP)
  administered by Universal Music Corp. (ASCAP)
This arrangement © 2016 Justin Hurwitz Music (BMI), Warner-Tamerlane Publishing Corp.
  (BMI), administered by Warner-Tamerlane Publishing Corp. (BMI), and B Lion Music (BMI)
  administered by Songs Of Universal, Inc. (BMI)/Pick In A Pinch Music (ASCAP), breathelike
  music (ASCAP), WC Music Corp. (ASCAP) administered by WC Music Corp. (ASCAP) and
  A Lion Music (ASCAP) administered by Universal Music Corp. (ASCAP)
All Rights Reserved   Used by Permission
Reprinted by permission of Hal Leonard LLC

The song reprises later in the film, this time as a duet between Mia and
Seb. It is the only song the two sing together while they are in love. Mia comes
home and hears Seb playing the piano, a slightly embellished, rubato version
of "City of Stars," but now diegetically grounded. He begins to sing along,
and Mia turns to watch and listen. The camera pans to Mia and then zooms
in on her, showing the slightly bittersweet smile on her face. Then she begins
to sing, walking toward Seb and leaning on the piano. The two share a very
genuine moment as she laughs slightly while singing, and they continue to

sing in duet, sitting next to each other on the piano bench while Seb plays along. The lyrics, about how "all we're looking for is love from someone else" and how the two characters are happy about this feeling and want it to stay, are perhaps the most earnest and cheerful of any song in the film thus far. Yet the music remains understated and melancholy throughout. After they have stopped singing, it continues with the orchestra gradually entering, and the image cuts to a montage of several big decisions Mia and Seb make that will ultimately destabilize their relationship: Seb signs a contract to work with Keith's band, and Mia quits her job at the coffee shop to focus on her one-woman show. As the montage continues, they are both seen pouring increasing attention into their individual pursuits, and therefore becoming increasingly isolated from each other. Mia is absorbed in writing her show, and Seb comes home from playing a concert after Mia has already gone to bed. Toward the end of the montage, Mia drives by the Rialto, where they had their first date, and notices it has closed. The scene ends with a dissolve back to Mia and Seb sitting at the piano, singing together and smiling, unaware of what is to come. During the song that encapsulates the most genuine moment of their expression of their love for each other, we essentially see through the montage how their relationship is about to dissolve.

As mentioned in Chapter 1, earlier versions of the script included a song called "La La Land" that was to represent, in Chazelle's words, "the high point of the romance . . . a number to enjoy the honeymoon, so to speak . . . right before stuff started to go wrong."[50] As the film went into prep, the song no longer seemed to fit. According to Chazelle, Ryan Gosling suggested a reprise of "City of Stars" in its place, even though it had never been intended as a duet. At the height of the couple's romance, instead of a high-energy love song, we already gain insight into the uncertainty that their relationship, or any relationship, will succeed. It's a message of doubt, where a classic Hollywood musical would have depicted love against all odds.

The Gene Kelly/MGM Spectacular: "Epilogue/Dream Ballet"

In the finale, titled "Epilogue," we see Mia and Seb imagine what their lives might have been like had they stayed together. The scene takes the form of a dream ballet, a flight of fancy conveyed visually through choreography, setting, and camera editing, accompanied by a medley of melodies heard throughout the film. Dream ballets—production numbers that convey meaning primarily through dance to further explore plot, themes, psychology, or emotions of the characters—were a fixture of many stage and screen musicals from the mid-20th century, beginning with Agnes de Mille's dream ballet for *Oklahoma!* in 1943.[51] Perhaps the most well-known onscreen examples are from the Gene Kelly MGM films *An American in Paris* (1951) and *Singin' in the Rain*, which are also the aesthetic references most explicitly drawn on in *La La Land*'s Epilogue. In both of these films' dream ballets, Kelly blended tap and ballet dance styles, staging an elaborate narrative related to the story (although only peripherally in *Singin' in the Rain*), with deliberately artificial sets and exaggerated color palettes, a nod to more avant-garde artistic practices within the popular genre of the film musical. These dream ballets are also somewhat more pessimistic or cynical in tone than the rest of the films they are part of, depicting romances that do not end happily. In the case of *La La Land*, Chazelle suggests that the Epilogue offers a chance to "re-watch the movie as though it were a musical that completely followed the old musical rules."[52] In so doing, it flips the dream ballet script, depicting an imagined happier version of the story than we see in the film's diegetic "real world."

In the Epilogue's imagined version of Mia and Seb's relationship, instead of Seb brushing Mia off the moment they see each other at the restaurant, he immediately embraces her, the camera's 360-degree tracking shot heightening the romance of the moment. Seb's boss forgives him for not sticking to the playlist; Seb waves Keith away without considering his request to play for the Messengers; Mia's one-woman show is a rousing success (and Seb is there in the audience cheering her on); and after Mia's successful audition (conveyed through shadow puppetry), the two go to Paris together while she shoots her film. At one point, they end up on a studio set, then walk through two-dimensional scenery, representing, in various degrees of abstraction, different settings they had encountered in real life, before they encounter people dancing on the freeway in an abstract reference to "Another Day of Sun." Throughout, the references to other films are frequent and numerous, creating an even more heightened sense of artificiality and abstraction, and further suggesting that this scene is not reality, but fantasy.

The section of the ballet that depicts their time in Paris is the most jam-packed with intertextual references. They end up at the Caveau de la Huchette jazz club, which is visually reminiscent of both the nightclub section of *Singin' in the Rain*'s "Broadway Melody" dream ballet and the jazz club section of the "Girl Hunt" dream ballet in *The Band Wagon*. Mia stands in front of a cardboard set of the Arc de Triomphe holding a bunch of balloons, a reference to the shot of Audrey Hepburn in front of the real Arc de Triomphe in *Funny Face* (1957). The two walk to an abstract set that depicts the banks of the Seine, a nod to several numbers from *An American in Paris*. They pass a boy holding a red balloon, referencing the French film *Le Ballon rouge* (1956); a couple on a park bench in the same embrace as Guy and Geneviève in *Les Parapluies de Cherbourg*; and then a man in an old-fashioned sailor uniform, a reference to the three U.S. Navy sailor characters in *On the Town* (1949). They then begin to waltz together, onto a dark set punctuated with star-like lights, a callback to the Planetarium scene but also a clear visual reference to Fred Astaire and Eleanor Powell's visually stunning choreography to "Begin the Beguine" on an equally stunning abstract set in *Broadway Melody of 1940* (1940).

The scene then cuts to Mia and Sebastian sitting in front of a home projector, watching home movies of this imagined version of their relationship through Mia's pregnancy, the birth of their baby, and the first couple years of the baby's life. Though this portion of the dream ballet does not reference any specific films, the image looks like it was shot in a Super 8 format, lending it an air of pastness and nostalgia. They leave their son with a babysitter, mirroring the same scene with Mia and her husband before the dream ballet, and they happen upon a jazz club and walk inside. There, they hear musicians play "Mia & Sebastian's Theme" before the scene reveals that Mia and Seb are back in their respective realities, Seb at the piano and Mia in the audience with her husband. Though the dream ballet began in an upbeat, playful fashion, the end is steeped in the melancholy and bittersweet feeling of missed chances and love lost, just like the dream ballet in *An American in Paris*, but without the happy union of the couple in the latter film's final minute.

Chazelle claims that he had wanted to include a dream ballet in a film musical since *Guy and Madeline*—the black-and-white film would have featured a dream ballet in color—but that resources did not allow it. But with the larger budget of *La La Land*, it was always a core element of the screenplay: "One of the main reasons I thought making a musical was worth the effort was to do a full-fledged dream ballet."[53] He liked the fact that it allowed "commercial Hollywood studio filmmaking" to engage with "really weird abstract avant-garde gestures."[54] Ultimately, the dream ballet allows for a theoretical, imagined interaction between Mia and Seb, "an entire narrative at the end, an entire emotionally satisfying reunion scene between them, basically, without a word of dialogue."[55] But that satisfying reunion is shattered when the two characters return to their realities. It is a nostalgic nod to older genres, while also poignantly hinting at what could have been for Mia and Seb.

The Many Meanings of Nostalgia

La La Land's intertextuality is multivalent. It serves to draw many spectators in through its unexpected juxtapositions. It pays homage to the films that inspired *La La Land*. It turns Mia and Seb's Los Angeles surroundings into a more fantastical, dreamlike place, one that heightens the stakes of their romance. The intertextual moments, throwbacks to bygone Hollywood, are also characterized by nostalgia. The references function on one level as an acknowledgment of the aesthetic debt that Chazelle and Hurwitz owe to earlier filmmakers, and, by extension, a desire to return to the aesthetic style of these films. If magical things could happen in early film musicals, why not try to recapture that magic?

La La Land's nostalgia has garnered both praise and criticism. For some audience members, the film's nostalgic impulses are part of its love letter to Hollywood, to classic films more generally, and to the film musical from its heyday. Louise Keller, for instance, called the film "an old-fashioned Hollywood musical that makes everything old new again" and wrote, "The setting is contemporary, the tone is timeless. . . . The way the past and the present fuse together while the real world fades into insignificance in the circular exposition is sheer brilliance . . . it's a breath of fresh air."[56] Likewise, Diane Garrett called the film "deceptively innovative," evoking "classic musicals while pushing the genre forward; it's old-fashioned and modern at the same time."[57] For critics like Keller and Garrett, its references to earlier films allowed *La La Land* to update the genre while paying homage to its history, and this was part of what made the film seem so novel and exciting, yet simultaneously almost timeless or out of time.

Others have seen the film's nostalgic approach as more problematic and backward-looking. At best, they see it as recycling without reinvention, and at worst, a longing for a time that may seem simpler for some but was characterized by marginalization and oppression of others. Richard Voeltz positions *La La Land*'s many intertextual references within the broader context of the immense popularity of remakes and reboots in the first decades of the 21st century, what he calls "mediated narcissistic nostalgia."[58] Geoff Nelson pointedly argues, in his polemically titled article "The Unbearable Whiteness of *La La Land*":

> Looking backwards with a romantic eye courts dangerous contemporary politics. What does Chazelle hope we see when we look back? . . . Why do white Americans (in politics and film) often so wistfully return to the era before federally mandated desegregation, voting and civil rights? . . . The film's politics of nostalgia and whiteness are inextricable. . . . *La La Land* isn't the escapism America needs right now, it's a regressive effort at time travel with no sense of shame for America's many historical sins.[59]

Nelson reminds us that the purported timelessness the film evokes is actually grounded in cinematic examples from a very specific time, one characterized by segregation, marginalization of people of color, and, I would add, rigid gender politics. Whether intended or not, the effect of incorporating nostalgic references to a past era of filmmaking is not as benign as it may initially seem.

Yet, within the story, Seb and Mia's nostalgia for older art is portrayed with a degree of critique. And because of the constant ways in which Chazelle and Hurwitz undercut, filter, or subvert the intertextual references, it is unclear just how literally to take the nostalgic impulses of the film. The references to past films are indeed a fundamental part of *La La Land*'s distinctive style. But the film is not a remake or a period piece. Instead, its blending of old and new—new in terms of both the story being told and the audiovisual style used to tell it—balances the nostalgia with a contemporary dose of reality. It remains ambiguous to what extent the updated approaches to the film musical found in *La La Land* end up critiquing or subverting its nostalgic impulses. Perhaps the fantastical settings of the older film musical, contrasted with *La La Land*'s contemporary realities, highlight the futility of the film musical genre's fantasy.

3

Modernizing a Classic Form

Realism and Virtuosic Performance

"People love what other people are passionate about," Mia says to Seb as he doubts whether his idea for a jazz club could ever succeed. But she doubts her own resolve to become a successful actress when she asks him, "What if I'm not good enough?" Though the narrative of *La La Land* focuses on the ups and downs of the romance between Mia and Seb, the main theme of the film—and the source of conflict both in their relationship and within each character—is the question of what it takes to stay true to one's dream. In the case of *La La Land*, both characters dream of being artists—Seb a jazz musician and Mia a movie actress. But how does one stay true to one's own artistic vision given the challenging realities of navigating the world as an artist in the 21st century? What sacrifices must you make? What compromises are necessary? How many setbacks are enough before the universe seems to be telling you to give up and try something else? According to the film's logic, Seb and Mia have to make a choice: between staying in their relationship and pursuing their dreams. Therefore, amidst the joyful whimsy brought about by the film musical mode of storytelling is a story steeped in 21st-century realism, in characters dealing with setbacks, disappointments, and compromise.

But, of course, no one *really* navigates the world singing and dancing. The film musical genre poses a unique challenge for filmmakers: how to reconcile the purported realism of cinema with the flights of fancy prompted by characters bursting into song and dance. As musical theater scholar Scott McMillin has claimed, there are two "orders of time" in the musical: book time and number time, with the latter granted special status.[1] No matter the particulars of a director's individual stylistic approach, musical numbers inevitably require a stylistic shift into a more fantastical mode of audiovisual expression. This is especially the case in the film musical. Compared to the abstraction of the stage, which automatically requires a certain suspension

La La Land. Hannah Lewis, Oxford University Press. © Oxford University Press 2024.
DOI: 10.1093/9780197682616.003.0004

of disbelief even in book time, cinema's ability to capture close-ups and subtle sounds makes it feel more realistic.[2] Cinematic number time therefore requires an even greater stylistic shift in order to be emotionally believable and justify the rupturing of cinematic realism.

In *La La Land*, Damien Chazelle sought to make what he called a "realist musical"; as a result, he intentionally cast leading actors who were inexperienced singers and dancers, opting for a raw, understated style of musical performance to create what he perceived as a more emotionally realistic performance style. As a result, every time expectations are built up for a transcendent musical moment, it is not the actors who deliver with exciting singing and dancing; instead, the spectacular effect of the film's musical moments is enlivened through the virtuosity of the camerawork and effects. The film's approach to technology can in part be understood as aligning with a broader stylistic trend in Hollywood films that features rapid editing, fragmentation, and free-ranging camerawork, cinematic visual techniques that have come to be an expected feature of contemporary cinema's audiovisual style.

This chapter explores the ways that the creative team's desire for realism is manifested in *La La Land*, a film that relies on the stylized audiovisual and narrative codes of classic Hollywood while depicting very modern relationship problems in a modern city. Because of the focus on realism in the depiction of Mia and Seb, there is something fundamentally different about the musical numbers in *La La Land* from those in the earlier films it attempts to emulate, particularly regarding the film's audiovisual syntax and its relationship between technology and performing onscreen bodies. I place some of *La La Land*'s most distinctive stylistic traits in the broader context of other contemporary film musicals that navigate similar challenges in a variety of ways. I also explore the concept of virtuosity in the film musical, arguing that technological virtuosity—what I call the "virtuosic camera"—often overshadows human virtuosity in *La La Land*, giving camerawork and editing style a privileged role over the performing bodies onscreen. This approach, I argue, suggests a contemporary discomfort with the emotional excess of singing and dancing onscreen, and reflects current anxieties about the relationship between human expression and technological virtuosity. The film's cinematography and realist narrative therefore reveal a very different side to *La La Land* than the nostalgic homage of its intertextual references explored in the previous chapter.[3]

Making a Musical "Realist"

La La Land embodies many of the tensions that come with the desire to make a film musical—a genre perceived as one of the most antirealist in film—realist. In some respects, Mia and Seb's relationship seems to come from a different time and place, a diegetic world that follows the antirealist logic of earlier film musicals. They burst into song and dance, spontaneously expressing their emotion in a syntax that is only acceptable in the diegetic world of a musical. Their choreographic style is of a different era, almost straight out of the 1940s or 1950s. Even their clothing nods to this earlier time, Seb with his tan wool suit and Mia with her vivid-colored, knee-length dresses and tap shoes.

At the same time, they are not fully or comfortably in this particular cinematic world either. Ryan Gosling and Emma Stone are not highly trained singers or dancers. Their vocal delivery and choreography are earnest, but rough around the edges. They are real people trying to navigate a diegetic world, steeped in older traditions, in which people sing and dance. As critic Alissa Wilkinson writes, "Gosling and Stone aren't the greatest at [singing or dancing]—notes fall flat, steps are a bit tentative—but that seems like the point: they're struggling, and success is in no way a guarantee."[4] As Chazelle put it to me, if regular people were to "start breaking into song or dance, there had to be this kind of humility to it."[5] This struggle, from both a narrative and an audiovisual stylistic standpoint, forms the basis of Chazelle's attempt to make a "realist musical," a fantastical, larger-than-life cinematic world that is simultaneously grounded in real-life problems and believable characters.

But the frame of the film is that of a traditional Hollywood musical in which leads could both act and sing (and often dance). The idea that a musical is more realist if the characters who are breaking into song and dance look and sound more like regular people is itself an artificial choice, intentionally working against the grain of the film musical's genre expectations. It implies that there is an inauthenticity of emotion if a film's narrative is interrupted by highly polished professional performances. Chazelle recounted to me that he and the actors "were certainly very aware, while making the movie and certainly while editing, that it's a musical that, at a certain point, kind of stops being a musical. Or at least puts it on pause, in a way that we knew might frustrate audiences, but was kind of part of the point."[6] Indeed, the film is front-loaded with songs, making the second half of the film feel more like a traditional cinematic drama. Chazelle's comment seems to suggest that, in spite of his attempt to reconcile the fantasy and artificiality of the film musical genre with realism, the two were ultimately incompatible.

Nevertheless, Chazelle claims he wanted to avoid what he called the "self-aware musical" that "had to apologize or explain for the fact that it was a musical." Instead, to him, the "essence of the genre was the complete lack of apology, the lack of explanation. The sort of defiance of it."[7] According to Chazelle, even though Gosling and Stone approached the script from a different perspective, drawn to a more "modern" (read: realist) approach, they all "liked this idea that there'd be an unspoken thing, maybe even just between their characters, that they kind of know they're in a musical . . . that the musical is a little bit the language of their love." He and the lead actors agreed that, even though they were explicitly avoiding irony, "everything [should] have an essential comic nature to it . . . that even when we were going to get into the deepest, darkest stuff, that this had to have a lightness of touch."[8] Additionally, although Chazelle claims that they intentionally cast actors who they would teach to sing and dance over singers or dancers they would teach to act, Stone and Gosling did go through rigorous singing and dance training, suggesting that these skills *were* at least somewhat important.

The film's approach to realism therefore contains a bundle of tensions and contradictions: the leading couple had to be realistic, portraying to the audience how "real people" might sound and look if they burst into song and dance, but at the same time they had to be somewhat self-aware of the artificiality of the mode of delivery in the narrative world of the film musical, one that most often features virtuosic singing and dancing. In the film musical, the tension in the space between everyday life and bursting into song creates what Scott McMillin calls a "crackle of difference,"[9] causing challenges for filmmakers, particularly those concerned with grounding their musicals in some semblance of realism. In the case of *La La Land*, it has implications both for the performance style of the actors and for the treatment of cinematic technology.

Technology, Virtuosity, and the Classic Hollywood Musical

Technological intervention has always been present in film musicals—from dubbing and post-synchronization, to editing together multiple takes of a complex dance number. Yet in film musicals of the Golden Age and even beyond, these technologies were typically rendered "transparent," to foreground the virtuosity of singing and dancing bodies and create a utopian world onscreen.[10] Fred Astaire famously wanted his dance numbers to be filmed in wide shots and long takes; he purportedly once said, "Either the camera will dance, or I will."[11] A classic Hollywood tactic was to make highly calculated and rehearsed numbers seem natural and unplanned, like the song "The Man That Got Away" in *A Star is Born* (1954), when Judy Garland is handed sheet music to a new song and seems to suddenly know all the words. In one of the most famous examples of movie musical technological trickery, Gene Kelly's iconic performance in the title song from *Singin' in the Rain* (1952) featured fake rain on a studio set resembling a Los Angeles street, and it required multiple takes shot over several days—all while Kelly was sick with a fever—in order to depict an impromptu exuberance that leads his character to sing and dance with abandon.[12] Though a product of intense behind-the-scenes labor, this scene appears to be a spontaneous expression of joy, a chance to show off Kelly's singular talent.

Even in numbers where the technological intervention was front and center, technological virtuosity was almost always presented to further highlight human virtuosity—a means of celebrating the magic of the movies alongside its most talented stars. As such, the numbers always bring the focus back to the virtuosity of the performer. Some of the most famous examples include Astaire's ceiling dance in *Royal Wedding* (1951), which involved a complex rotating set to make it appear as if he was dancing on the walls and ceiling; his flying sequence in "Seeing's Believing" in *The Belle of New York* (1952), where he floats in the air, appears to dance precariously atop the Washington Square arch, and then suddenly weightlessly dances alongside it; and Kelly's dance with animated partner Jerry of *Tom and Jerry* in *Anchors Aweigh* (1945), where real man and drawn mouse seamlessly respond to each other's movements. These kinds of numbers reflexively highlight cinematic technology not to "distanciate" the spectator in a Brechtian manner, but instead, according to Jane Feuer, as a means of "remystification" of performance and celebration of community onscreen, ultimately reifying the film musical as entertainment.[13] *Singin' in the Rain* is perhaps the best known example of this: the film seemingly pulls back the curtain on the process of dubbing, only to conceal its own participation in the very practice.[14] These uses of technology helped establish the musical numbers as special, fantastical utopic spaces where seemingly superhuman feats, enabled through technology, helped convey very human emotions.

Intensified Continuity and the Resurgence of the Film Musical

This relationship between the Hollywood musical genre, film technology, and audiovisual narrative style shifted after the Golden Age. Almost since the genre's beginnings, the film musical has been seen as a genre in decline, in need of resurrection.[15] The musical's unabashed embrace of fantasy worlds where characters burst into spontaneous song and dance became increasingly challenging for filmmakers to reconcile with technological developments and evolving cinematic expectations of realism. As Raymond Knapp has pointed out, the 1960s and 1970s marked a particularly fraught moment for the film musical, as "new standards and rationales for filmic realism" developed and filmmakers struggled to position musical numbers within a domain of realism. Knapp suggests, "In creating a specifically filmic sense of reality, film adaptations of musicals often foreclosed a central function of their songs, which, rather than establishing the 'real,' often appeared as artificial intrusions within the realities established according to more basic filmic conventions."[16] With the rapid changes in Hollywood's studio system and cinematic style in the 1960s, film musicals had to adapt their style to be perceived as relevant. Kelly Kessler has also pointed out that social and cinematic developments of the 1960s made it increasingly difficult for filmmakers and audiences to embrace the utopian world of the film musical, resulting in more ambivalent narratives.[17] The social unrest of the 1960s and subsequent cynicism of the 1970s and 1980s made the nostalgic project of the film musical sit uncomfortably with Hollywood's ever-changing cinematic priorities. Furthermore, the 1980s marked, according to John Muir, "the beginning of the blockbuster era when book musicals couldn't compete."[18]

But since the beginning of the 21st century, Hollywood has seen a resurgence of the movie musical genre, kicked off by the massive successes of *Moulin Rouge!* (2001) and *Chicago* (2002) in close succession.[19] The critical and audience reception of these two films opened the floodgates: soon after, a number of Broadway stage musicals were adapted for the screen, with notable examples including *Phantom of the Opera* (2004), *Rent* (2005), *Dreamgirls* (2006), *Sweeney Todd: The Demon Barber of Fleet Street* (2007), *Les Misérables* (2012), *Into the Woods* (2014), *Cats* (2019), *In the Heights* (2021), and *West Side Story* (2021). Jukebox musicals, or musicals featuring existing popular songs, have also been popular, including films like *Across the Universe* (2007) and *Rocketman* (2019), as well as *Moulin Rouge!* The 2007 film musical *Enchanted* was a different kind of adaptation: a parody and homage to Disney animated fairy tales, it featured both classic-style animation and contemporary-set live-action sequences. Since the mid-2010s, another trend has emerged: that of the live-action remake of animated films from the Disney Renaissance of the 1990s, including *Beauty and the Beast* (2017), *Aladdin* (2019), *The Lion King* (2019), and *The Little Mermaid* (2023). *La La Land* and the 2017 film *The Greatest Showman* have perhaps signaled something new for the genre, as both were completely original screenplays, not based on an existing stage production or film, and featured newly composed songs.

All of these films seem to signal a renaissance for the Hollywood musical, but with distinctly 21st-century sensibilities—the content is often darker and more realist, much in the same way that Broadway stage musicals have dealt with heavier subject matters in recent decades. Likewise, the audiovisual style of the film musical has shifted to reflect the technological advances and resulting stylistic evolution of contemporary cinema. At the same time, because film musicals in the 21st century remain relatively rare compared to other genres, each time a new musical is produced, it automatically enters a discourse about its break with or continuation of the genre's traditions. As a result, nostalgia for Golden Age Hollywood musicals is almost always on display, whether intentional or not. As cinema entered a new technological era, both original film musicals and adaptations have contended in different ways with nostalgia, referencing older forms and styles while also relying on new technology and contemporary cinematic techniques to update the genre and make it feel relevant to contemporary audiences.

But the incorporation of contemporary cinematic techniques has resulted in fundamental changes to the genre. In musicals produced since 2000, technological virtuosity often purposefully and overtly overshadows human virtuosity, with camerawork taking precedence over the coherent presentation of performing bodies. This shift is part of contemporary Hollywood's broader trend toward a new kind of audiovisual syntax that Carol Vernallis calls "accelerated aesthetics," a new presentation of "forms of space, time, and rhythm" in contemporary cinema and digital media.[20] David Bordwell calls this stylistic shift "intensified continuity," a visual style that involves fast cutting, fragmentation of the body in rapid edits, bipolar extremes of lens length, close framings in dialogue scenes, and a free-ranging camera.[21] When there are longer takes, according to Bordwell, "the camera is usually in motion," often creating "virtuoso shots" that track a character moving along a lengthy path.[22] Contemporary Hollywood cinema also frequently incorporates CGI (computer-generated imagery), blurring the line between animation and live action and creating humanly impossible visual effects. Some scholars have even suggested that a whole new "postclassical" style emerged toward the end of the 20th century, a distinct break from the narrative-driven classical Hollywood, perhaps most exemplified in recent blockbuster action films. As Geoff King suggests, blockbusters are designed to be spectacular, and "rapid editing and camera movement have become important sources of heightened spectacular impact in contemporary Hollywood . . . designed to create an impression of subjective immersion in the action."[23] The rapid, disorienting postmodern editing style of MTV music videos has also influenced the new approaches to musical numbers in narrative feature films.[24]

When incorporated into the aesthetic of the film musical, the audio-visual syntax of intensified continuity and accelerated aesthetics fragments the singing and dancing body, de-emphasizing the virtuosity of individual performers in the process. Indeed, the fragmentation of the performing body in the contemporary Hollywood musical is so pervasive that it seems to signal a broader phenomenon at play: a discomfort with the display of singing and dancing on screen. The cinematography attempts to mitigate the affective impact of musical performances, in a cynicism that reflects an unwillingness to accept virtuosic singing and dancing on its own terms. Instead, alternating between the hyperrealism of long traveling shots and the fragmented aesthetic of the music video, the virtuosic *camera* becomes the star, resting only briefly on the requisite singers or dancers in any given musical number.

Moulin Rouge! was the first film musical to overtly experiment with many of these audiovisual features of intensified continuity. Director Baz Luhrmann's postmodern, hyperrealistic style was very new at the time, and the cinematography as a result brazenly drew attention to itself.[25] In drawing on pre-existing popular music, the songs in *Moulin Rouge!* did not emulate classic Hollywood musical style. Instead, the popular songs were remixed and rearranged in a manner that fit closely with the film's visual style, placing its lineage as much in the MTV music video tradition of the 1980s as in that of the film musical. As a self-conscious element of the film's storytelling, the virtuosic camera was a means of brashly exposing the artificiality of the film musical genre. Many films have since adopted aspects of *Moulin Rouge!*'s visual style, but without the same kind of self-conscious reflexivity, resulting in an uneasy tension between their nostalgic projects and their technological virtuosity. This tension plays out in a number of contemporary Hollywood films, and it is displayed in very particular ways in *La La Land.*

Nostalgia, Technology, and the Virtuosic Camera in *La La Land*

La La Land's technologies demonstrate the tension between nostalgia and realism that runs through the film. On the one hand, they pay homage to mid-century Hollywood. *La La Land* was shot on film, rather than digitally (even though it would have been projected digitally at most movie theaters), with Panavision equipment in a 2.55:1 widescreen format, the aspect ratio made famous by CinemaScope. CinemaScope was a filmmaking process used from the mid-1950s to the mid-1960s to project a film in widescreen. Films like *Rebel Without a Cause* (1955), *The King and I* (1956), and *The Seven Year Itch* (1955) were presented in CinemaScope; many other film musicals of the 1950s and 1960s experimented with other widescreen formats that are no longer in regular use today. *La La Land* opens with a black-and-white title that clearly announces its technological debt to earlier eras: "Presented in CinemaScope."[26] At first, it is in a narrow format, the title cut off on both sides, before the screen broadens to the familiar widescreen format and dissolves into color, showing the full old-fashioned CinemaScope logo. Beginning in a narrow format in black-and-white seems to initially place the film in an even older era, while the widening into the CinemaScope aspect ratio feels like an opening up—now we can see events unfold in rich, saturated color and widescreen! This explicit call-out to a now-vintage technology serves as a symbolic filter that encourages audiences to understand the narrative as somehow emanating from a particular time and place, while making the modern visual and narrative markers even more striking by contrast.

But when it comes to cinematography, though the influences might have been vintage, the visual style of the musical numbers reveals contemporary sensibilities. Chazelle claims to have approached *La La Land* with the notion that "musical numbers, especially dance numbers, just tended to be better when they were not cut."[27] Perhaps responding to values perpetuated by figures like Astaire and Kelly, who wanted to prove that their dancing was not faked by body doubles, Chazelle likened minimal cutting to classic Hollywood aesthetic sensibilities. This idea was in contrast with his approach to *Whiplash*: he formulated an idea in his mind that his earlier film was

> where I'd go nuts with the cutting, and *La La Land* would be where I go nuts with the camera movement and the oners [one-shot scenes]. And it made sense in my mind because *Whiplash*—I always thought of it as about

right angles and straight lines. And it was this idea of the metronome and the bars of music. And you're either on tempo or off tempo, on time [or] off time. So that made sense. And then, *La La Land* had to be romantic and dance. It had to be dance. So it was all going to be curves, it was all going to be circles. And so . . . things that tie those two styles together would be things like, within a oner, fast pans between one element or the other.[28]

But the nature of the long shots found in many of the film's musical numbers is quite different from those in classic Hollywood musicals. Extensive traveling shots and whip pans are prominent cinematic features in several *La La Land* songs, perhaps most notably in "Another Day of Sun," where a traffic jam on the Los Angeles freeway spontaneously evolves into an ebullient and virtuosic ensemble performance. As I described in Chapter 2, the scene fulfills many of the functions of a classic opening number: it establishes setting, community, and a world where characters express themselves through song. Impressively, the scene appears to be filmed in a single take, the extended traveling shot a feat of cinematic virtuosity that leaves spectators thinking, "How did they *do* that?"

Technology abounds in this number: in a final stunning visual, we see what appears to be hundreds of dancers standing on their cars doing the same choreography down to the end of the freeway entrance. In reality, there were only thirty dancers in the scene; CGI was used to fill in the rest of the dancers. Perhaps more significantly, this scene is a quintessential example of what Bordwell calls a "virtuoso shot,"[29] filmed to appear as if it is done in a single take, and requiring untold stamina—and a little bit of luck—from its large ensemble cast of singers and dancers. But cinematic sleight of hand was used to create the virtuosic camera effect in this scene: in reality, three carefully timed whip pans allowed for seamless cutting of three distinct shots. In an interview, choreographer Mandy Moore suggested, "We knew we needed to create movement that would inform an edit," and she shaped the choreography around these whip pans.[30] Though choreographers for stage and screen have always had to consider the constraints of their medium—from issues of space and visibility onstage to the framing of the camera—Moore's comment indicates that the virtuoso traveling shot was the primary structuring focus of the scene, a self-conscious display of the creative team's technological prowess.

This use of the virtuosic camera to capture mass movement does have precedent in the elaborate choreographic sequences of Busby Berkeley's films of the 1930s. Berkeley's numbers often brazenly exploited the camera to create seemingly impossible angles and shapes with his chorus girls. Pamela Robertson suggests that Berkeley "offers a purely cinematic vision of entertainment in which the camera itself dances and the spectator identifies with its movements, rather than with characters who sing and dance."[31] The historical precedent of Berkeley's choreography is instructive. Berkeley's choreography has been interpreted in a number of ways: as commentary on industrialization, as an extravagance offered as an escapist antidote to the hardship of the Great Depression, and as feminist camp, for instance.[32] Just like Berkeley's numbers, in "Another Day of Sun," the big-picture sequence takes precedence over the showcasing of any of the individuals onscreen. What differentiates this number from those in Berkeley's films is that it seems to offer the *promise* of individual opportunities to shine—instead of being dressed uniformly, each character brings a different costume, personality, and singing voice to the table. But each performer is given very brief screen time to feature their singing or dancing before the camera moves on to the next person, and we frequently do not see the person's whole body, just a portion of it; the camera is dancing more than the characters, even as they perform their individualized choreography (Figures 3.1a–f). As a result, the virtuoso shot becomes the most memorable aspect of the scene's movement, causing the individuality of each performer to be glossed over.

The downplaying of human virtuosity in favor of the virtuosic camera is also apparent in the leading couple's duet at the Griffith Observatory. In this scene, Mia and Seb dance together to symbolize finally having fallen in love. Just as Fred Astaire and Vera-Ellen floated above the buildings in *The Belle of New York*, revealing their feelings of love for each other, Seb and Mia float effortlessly off the ground to dance among the stars. Yet the moment their dance (literally) gets off the ground, the CGI effects take over, remaining the focus of the scene as the characters float in the air (Figure 3.2). The couple's synchronized movements remain simple and understated. In contrast with the 1930s dance duets of Astaire and Rogers, who are seen as a perfect match in their films because of how seamlessly they dance together, Mia and Seb's romance requires digital special effects to unite the couple in dance, perhaps an early sign that the two are destined not to end up together.[33] The scene's editing style—the need for CGI to artificially bring the couple together— belies its own nostalgia for romantic courtship symbolized through dance.

One major exception to this approach in the film is Mia's solo number, "Audition (The Fools Who Dream)." Though the virtuosic camera is still

Figures 3.1a–f "Another Day of Sun," *La La Land*

Figure 3.2 Planetarium Scene, *La La Land*

active, it is used in tandem with Stone's performance, to different effect. This number is a raw, heartfelt, intensely personal number that reveals Mia's acting abilities and leads her to land a part in a movie that jumpstarts her career as a successful actress. The two casting directors sit behind a table and ask her to tell them a story. She begins to describe her aunt, who once jumped in the Seine when she was in Paris. Her aunt's experiences encouraged Mia to chase her dreams, no matter how foolish: "Here's to the ones who dream/ Foolish as they may seem/Here's to the hearts that ache/Here's to the mess we make." The audition room and casting directors seem to disappear as the room fades to black, with only Mia illuminated. She begins telling her story, then slowly transitions to singing, at first a cappella. A piano enters underneath, and the accompaniment slowly builds up as the orchestra joins and the song builds in intensity. Visually, the song is filmed in one continuous take, beginning with a very slow zoom into a close-up of Mia's face (Figure 3.3), then a slow arc shot around her, and concluding with a slow zoom out. As the song concludes, the audition room comes back into focus, and we see the backs of the casting directors watching her performance. Emma Stone's vocals were not postsynchronized, but rather recorded live on set to Justin Hurwitz's piano accompaniment.[34] Though the camerawork is impressive, it is clearly designed to highlight the virtuosity of Stone's performance—that of her singing, but more notably, her acting. This number, unlike most others in the film, incorporates technology at the service of displaying raw, human—realist—emotion. It reveals an alternative means of combining contemporary audiovisual technology and the presentation of singing onscreen, one that does not shy away from earnest musical expression.

Figure 3.3 "Audition," *La La Land*

Interestingly, the audiovisual style of Mia's audition song is not emulated in any of the film's other songs. In fact, the musical numbers seemed to pose a "problem" for the realist sensibilities of the film. Chazelle once admitted that "at some point—I don't mean all at once—but we tried at different points cutting every [musical] number from the movie."[35] Though the film's creative team was working hard to make sure each number aided the storytelling, this fact perhaps also indicates their overall discomfort with how best to present singing and dancing onscreen, especially in the context of realism.[36] Rather than eschew fantasy entirely, the film relies on visual feats of technology, which perhaps feels more "realistic" in the context of contemporary cinema than the unabashed and emotional bursting into song and dance.

The Virtuosic Camera in Other Contemporary Film Musicals

The virtuosic camera seems to be present to different degrees in almost every contemporary film musical, though with a range of aesthetic results. *The Greatest Showman* and *In the Heights* provide two helpful points of both comparison and contrast to illustrate the extent to which *La La Land*'s audiovisual aesthetic is part of a broader trend in contemporary film musicals. A year after *La La Land*'s release, *The Greatest Showman* became the fifth-highest-grossing non-animated film musical, following on *La La Land*'s heels in its commercial success and trend of paying homage to the classics of the genre. Director Michael Gracey got his start shooting commercials and music videos, and in the film's musical numbers, the postmodern music video aesthetic is fully on display, in combination with a cinematographic style that seems like it would be at home in a contemporary action film. A sense of the epic and otherworldly is created by fragmenting of the actors' bodies through rapid editing, dizzying arc shots, and experimentation with camera speed and other special effects.

In the number "Rewrite the Stars," for instance, the film's heartfelt love song between an African American acrobat (Zendaya) and the wealthy white socialite Philip Carlyle (Zac Efron), the camera rarely shows the characters in close-up as they are singing; instead, we see a complex acrobatic choreography as the two characters soar in the air, to the sounds of their autotuned voices and a highly layered conventional pop accompaniment. This stunning visual sequence is cut up by frequent edits and extended arc shots, visually dazzling but emotionally understated because of its focus on the virtuosic camera. At least one stunt double was used for Efron's acrobatics in this scene, which partially explains the need for such frequent editing.[37] Yet, rather than being a tool to display the heightened emotions of the characters, the camerawork draws attention to its own visual spectacle. When we finally do see the couple in close-up together, their faces are in shadow, as the editing style again avoids even a brief earnest declaration of love between the two characters, as would be found in traditional love songs in Golden Age film musicals.

The fragmentation of performers' bodies is apparent even in one of the more modest musical numbers, the duet "The Other Side" with Hugh Jackman (as P. T. Barnum) and Efron. In the song, Barnum tries to convince Carlyle to fund his circus, despite the society man's reservations about how his peers would perceive his involvement in such unrefined entertainment. The two men are alone in a bar, sitting next to each other and drinking, as the bartender pours them drink after drink. The camera begins by following the movement of the liquor bottle as Barnum grabs it from the bartender, pours them shots, and passes it back to the bartender, who has moved to the other side of the bar. As the song approaches the chorus, the two men spin around in their barstools, and the camera cuts 180 degrees on the downbeat, then spins around as Jackman begins to dance around the bar. His dance, however, is never fully captured in any single camera shot, because the camera cuts to a close-up of his feet as they move, then back to a medium long shot, then quickly to Efron's reaction shot. Both Efron and Jackman are highly trained musical performers, but their voices and lyrics are obscured in the heavily mixed audio track, and their choreography is chopped up by camera movement that seems to intentionally disorient the spectator's sense of space.

The 2021 film adaptation of *In the Heights* made greater attempts to reconcile contemporary cinematic techniques with earnest expression of performance. Perhaps the film's subject matter required it: the story focuses on the individual trials and tribulations of members of a predominantly Latinx community in Manhattan's Washington Heights neighborhood, a community that has typically been ignored in popular culture representation. Regardless of the reason, it is clear that director John Chu incorporated many aspects of intensified continuity (rapid cutting, whip pans, CGI, and animation overlaid over live action) into his cinematic style to heighten the film's fantasy, while never taking the focus away from the main characters and their genuine, heartfelt expression of emotions: "We want it to feel like a vintage musical that you found, but done in a way that was never made back then," claimed Chu.[38] One example is the song "When the Sun Goes Down," sung by characters Nina and Benny. The two characters sing to each other on a fire escape, then suddenly appear to defy gravity, dancing on the side of a building. Chu and cinematographer Alice Brooks explicitly cited Fred Astaire's number from *Royal Wedding* as a source of inspiration, and in fact used the same trick of a rotating set. The first minute and a half of the scene was intentionally shot with no cuts, to highlight the fact that the shift in gravity was accomplished without CGI or dance doubles. At the same time, the scene could not have been shot without contemporary cinematic techniques, particularly CGI, which was utilized to overlay the actors with the outdoor cityscape at sunset (in reality shot separately weeks before). Nevertheless, the virtuosic camerawork is not compensatory, but instead complements the skills of the performers: the song's focus is on the emotional reason for their seeming weightlessness, and on the ease with which the performers dance their emotions, just like Astaire's number seventy years earlier.[39] The combination of older and newer cinematographic "tricks" ultimately aids in delivering a heartfelt love song, where the actors' skilled voices and nimble movements are equally on display.

The Tension of Old and New

Just as *La La Land*'s audiovisual style blends old and new, combining classic visual filmmaking techniques (CinemaScope; a rich, saturated color palette) with contemporary cinematography, the film also blends realism and fantasy in a manner that creates interesting tensions and challenges in presenting the narrative. Its use of the virtuosic camera alongside the rawer, realer performance styles of the lead actors shows how these competing impulses are sometimes uncomfortably juxtaposed in the film, in ways both intentional and perhaps unintentional. What is clear is that *La La Land* is not the only film musical of the 21st century to grapple with this aesthetic juxtaposition.

The shift in the film musical's audiovisual syntax that I have described has received mixed reactions. Some audiences and critics have found it troubling, expecting that singing and dancing should be the main source of the cinematic spectacle in a film musical, but not all audiences approach it with these preconceived notions of the genre. Others have been captivated by the cinematic style of recent Hollywood musicals, finding magic and wonder in the visual effects of CGI and the virtuosic camera. As audiences have become accustomed to CGI and intensified continuity through contemporary blockbuster action and fantasy films, their presence in other genres no longer seems unusual or jarring, even in a musical film. Indeed, the emphasis on the virtuosic camera can move the audience in a different way by leaving them in awe and drawing them into the realm of fantasy. But the different approach to human and cinematic virtuosity from the genre's Golden Age predecessors is symptomatic of broader cultural and artistic shifts. Whether we consider the contemporary film musical's audiovisual syntax to be a distinct shift away from earlier styles or an updated technological means of serving the same end, it is worth exploring the implications of this focus on technology over human performance.

In his landmark essay "Entertainment and Utopia," Richard Dyer claims that musicals respond to real needs or problems in society and offer onscreen utopian solutions to those problems. So what needs are contemporary filmmakers responding to? What does the film musical in the age of intensified continuity tell us about our particular cultural moment? If Busby Berkeley's fragmenting of the female chorus girl in the 1930s was an oblique comment on the dehumanization of the machine age and the Great Depression, then we can certainly find similar resonances in our contemporary moment. In their audiovisual style, contemporary Hollywood musicals reflect current anxieties about the relationship between human expression and technological virtuosity, between the draw of the past and the promise of the future. The mixed reception of many of these films may in part be because of these anxieties. In an era of autotune, CGI, and artificial intelligence, human virtuosity—even basic human expression—is more difficult to pinpoint onscreen and on the soundtrack. How can we, as viewers, trust what we see and hear if we are so highly aware of the manipulation that goes into it? Or, perhaps more concerning, what do we make of the fact that audiences are often unaware of this frequent manipulation of sound or image in the first place? The use of CGI to create the illusion of dancers in *La La Land* also connects to contemporary anxieties surrounding automation and the politics of labor—of computer graphics taking away potential roles from extras, much in the same way that people have decried the trend toward replacing live musicians with synthesizers and recordings in Broadway pit orchestras.[40]

La La Land's nostalgia for the golden age of the film musical sits in uneasy tension with this technological ambivalence, providing insight into some of the anxieties of our current cultural moment, our desire to delight in the past while acknowledging its problematic aspects in our contemporary digital age. The film seems to challenge its own premise, continually questioning to what extent we should relish in the moments of nostalgia, and to what extent we should embrace the new.

4

La La Land and Jazz

Seb and Mia are strolling together on the Warner Bros. backlot, their chemistry becoming apparent. Suddenly, Mia looks over to him and confesses her feelings: "I should probably tell you something now. Just to get it out of the way. I hate jazz." Seb stops in his tracks. "What do you mean you hate jazz?" He then takes it upon himself to change her mind. The next scene, Seb takes Mia to hear a jazz combo at the Lighthouse Café and recounts the genre's history and context to her, hoping to convey what he finds so exciting about it. Mia responds with clichéd resistance: "But what about Kenny G?" and "Where I grew up . . . people would just put on [the jazz radio station] when they had a cocktail party, and everyone would kind of just talk over it." In a desperate attempt to reach Mia, Seb describes what they are listening to as "conflict and compromise," as "new, every time. . . . It's very, very exciting." The combo ends their song, and Seb applauds emphatically, then turns to Mia and says gravely, "And it's dying. It's dying, Mia. It's dying on the vine. And the world says, 'Let it die. It had its time.' Well, not on my watch."

This scene establishes the centrality of jazz to *La La Land*'s story. By the time Chazelle directed *La La Land*, he had already written and directed two films with jazz musician protagonists (*Guy and Madeline on a Park Bench* and *Whiplash*), informed by his own background and experience as a jazz drummer. *La La Land* likewise made jazz an important part of both its soundscape and its narrative. Jazz permeates Justin Hurwitz's score, and there are several diegetic numbers played by jazz musicians onscreen. Additionally, Sebastian's identity is in large part defined by his relationship to the genre, as a jazz pianist eager to open his own club someday. His ability to make Mia understand why he is so passionate about jazz, and her embrace of the genre over the course of the film, symbolizes just how much they have grown as individuals during their relationship.

But jazz is additionally thematized in a way that sets it apart from Chazelle's earlier jazz-focused films, as the characters debate its very relevance as a musical genre. The jazz narrative is closely entwined with the film's nostalgia, making explicit some of the inherent stylistic tensions that were explored in

La La Land. Hannah Lewis, Oxford University Press. © Oxford University Press 2024.
DOI: 10.1093/9780197682616.003.0005

Chapters 2 and 3. Sebastian's view of jazz is decidedly nostalgic, as he clings to a moment in the genre's history—what he would consider its heyday—that predates his birth. As such, Sebastian laments that the genre is dying and takes it upon himself to "save" it, but his definition of jazz is decidedly narrow, to the point of being reactionary. He cannot accept the idea of the genre evolving to meet the tastes of contemporary audiences, and he feels he is "selling out" when he goes on tour with Keith (John Legend), a musician who has embraced a commercially successful fusion of jazz and popular music. Indeed, Seb embodies a debate that has long preoccupied the jazz world, between "purists" and those who embrace fusion or other evolutions of the genre. The intersections of race and genre in the jazz subplot make this debate particularly fraught in the film. In fact, the jazz narrative is the aspect where *La La Land*'s centering of white perspectives and experience, and therefore its broader racial problematic, becomes most clearly apparent.

In this chapter, I delve into the film's ambivalence about jazz: its stylistic boundaries; who gets to play it; and who, if anyone, gets to "save" it. I additionally discuss the character of Keith as portrayed by John Legend, the kind of approach to jazz he represents, and the differences between the depiction of contemporary jazz fusion in the film and the jazz renaissance that was actually taking place in Los Angeles right around the time of *La La Land*'s production. I argue that the film's ambivalence leaves its message about jazz open to interpretation. On the one hand, by connecting the (largely) white genre of the Hollywood musical with the historically Black genre of jazz, *La La Land* participates in a long history of racial masquerading in the Hollywood musical. On the other hand, by portraying Seb's desire to "save" jazz with some degree of critique, it undercuts its own parallel nostalgic agenda for the film musical.

Sebastian as Gatekeeper: The Boundaries of Jazz in *La La Land*

Jazz is in many ways the dominant musical language of *La La Land*. Its jazz-inflected songs and score connect to its nostalgia for an earlier era of film musicals, much like its visual and narrative references. Indeed, from the film musical genre's beginnings in the late 1920s until the mid-20th century, jazz and the film musical were very closely connected. Jazz was an important genre in American popular music at the time, and its stylistic markers can be found in the songs and scores of countless musicals, on both stage and screen. Influential composers for musical theater and film, such as George Gershwin and Irving Berlin, intentionally incorporated musical features associated with jazz into their songs, many of which later became the backbone of the Great American Songbook, a loosely defined group of songs that comprise today's jazz standards. According to Chazelle, he and Hurwitz always envisioned that *La La Land*'s score would have elements of jazz in it, as a means of connecting the film to its cinematic predecessors: "There's obviously elements of jazz in it; it's what happened to the American Songbook. . . . It all began with jazz."[1] Chazelle's comment represents a reductive view of the stylistic origins of the film musical and the Great American Songbook, ignoring the range of American and European popular music styles and traditions that fed into them, including operetta, ballads, march songs, and waltzes. Nevertheless, his remarks reveal the extent to which his and Hurwitz's understanding of the close connection between jazz and the film musical informed their conception of *La La Land*'s musical style.

But Sebastian would be hard pressed to see things the same way. Although many of his heroes engaged with songs from musicals (John Coltrane's "My Favorite Things," for instance), he would look upon Hollywood musicals' connection to jazz with disdain. His definition of jazz is fixed in the past, as revealed by his actions throughout the film, but it is a myopic view. He obsessively listens to and then plays along with a several-bar passage from Thelonious Monk's "Japanese Folk Song." He chides his sister for sitting on Hoagy Carmichael's stool. He laments the closing of the fictional Van Beek jazz club, which has been turned into a "samba-tapas place." As a musician, he mostly plays in a post-bop or hard bop style of the 1950s and 1960s. And throughout the film, he is consistently resistant to updating, modernizing, or diluting the genre from the particular styles that he champions in his own playing. As I discuss later in this chapter, he is depicted in stark opposition to Keith, who has found an audience and financial success playing a jazz-inflected popular style of music. Seb, on the other hand, reaches the apex of his version of success at the end of the film by opening a vintage jazz club.

Because Sebastian is the male protagonist, in his attempts to draw boundaries around what does or does not count as jazz, his voice is elevated above all others in the film. However, he represents only one specific understanding of the genre. Indeed, in voicing his opinions about jazz, he ends up echoing the arguments of one side of the "jazz wars" that took place among critics and fans during the second half of the 20th century. Jazz has been debated and contested almost since its beginnings.[2] But as rock became the dominant popular music style in the 1960s and 1970s, jazz musicians and critics began to advocate for jazz as a "legitimate" artistic genre, attaching more value to it through its perceived respectability.[3] By the 1980s, in many people's eyes, jazz had become, according to critic Nate Chinen, "synonymous with respectability. . . . It was staunchly historical, endlessly concerned with recapturing the mood of 1959, or 1963."[4] Any attempt to blend jazz with rock or other popular genres was met with resistance by purists who saw it as a form of "selling out."[5] Although musical mixture was nothing new, this instance of it generated a particularly polarizing critical response because jazz was understood as diametrically opposed to rock and funk. Seve Chambers points to the fact that "for at least the past 30 years, musicians of the neo-bop movement have bemoaned the addition of rock and hip-hop into the genre . . . seeing it as a death knell for the purity of their music."[6] Sebastian's understanding of jazz therefore embodies one side of a discourse in jazz circles that had become tired and well worn (albeit still resonant for some) by the 21st century.

Sebastian further embodies a jazz stereotype that Chinen playfully calls the "jazzbro." The jazzbro, according to Chinen, "is a self-styled jazz aficionado, overwhelmingly male and usually a musician in training himself . . . [who exploits] jazz knowledge as a private commodity selectively put on public display. . . . Like the Cold War hipster, the contemporary jazzbro is utterly convinced of both the superiority of his taste and the marginalization of his ideas."[7] The jazzbro becomes a musical gatekeeper, making jazz seem esoteric and out of reach for many, which, according to David A. Graham, "poses a serious challenge to jazz's ongoing health."[8] Indeed, Seb's monologue to Mia about jazz epitomizes the jazzbro mentality. She espouses decidedly stereotypical views about jazz: that it is easy listening, that it is cocktail music to talk over, and that it has no relevance to her life.[9] In response, Seb mansplains jazz to her, recounting a romanticized history of its origins and describing what makes it so exciting while dismissing her understandings of the genre. He refuses to acknowledge the validity of her experience of jazz, and although he laments the "dying" of the genre, he seems to have no perception that his point of view might be alienating to potential future jazz fans.

Chazelle claims that Seb's character as an uncompromising jazzbro seemed to more easily "fit in a musical":

To me, the type of characters that fit best in a musical are people who live in a little bit of a dream world—that that's where the language of the musical makes sense. If you can believe that your drum set is, you know, Jo Jones's drum set from a 1930s Kit Kat club in Kansas City, maybe you can believe that you can break into song and float up into the stars and stuff, the same kind of suspension from reality. And the strength of your own inner beliefs, divorced from reality. That was a little bit what was necessary for him.[10]

Sebastian's obsession with mid-century jazz perhaps reveals him as a dreamer with his head in the clouds, one who might be able to express himself through the song-and-dance language of the film musical. But if Seb's perspective on jazz was meant to show that he was living in a dream world, within the story of the film, he is never forced to wake up from that dream.

Seb's mentality was also in part autobiographical for Chazelle, which the director clearly feels ambivalent about. He admits that Sebastian is "kind of a parody of aspects of myself," but more so an "affectionate parody" of the kind of person he would meet as a jazz musician growing up, who would be "so obsessed with this little terrain of land that had little to do with his existence":

> If you look at it from outside, you're ridiculous. You're completely ridiculous. Why are you so anti this? Why are you acting like you're the guardian of this? You don't even have the life experience to really tie yourself to that in a deep way. At the same time, it's not completely a condemnation of that kind of character, either, because I also feel like the love of the art form is true and genuine, and there's something moving in that, especially love for an art form that's not going to give you much love in return.[11]

(Hurwitz, for his part, says that this aspect of the story "never resonated" with him.[12]) Seb's focus on past iterations of a genre that has in reality continued to evolve is another manifestation of the film's nostalgia. But the logic of the film never truly forces Seb to confront the ambivalence that Chazelle describes, and as a result, his jazzbro mentality is largely left unchallenged.

Sebastian as Jazz Savior: The Racial Politics of *La La Land*

The jazzbro is not just gendered, he is also racially marked. Chazelle himself was aware of this fact, noting, "The type of jazz snob [that Seb is a parody of] tends to be white. . . . It's someone who wouldn't claim it, but he implicitly assumes a kind of ownership of an art form that he can't really. And . . .

there's a little bit of a deep-down knowledge of that, and a little bit of a chip on the shoulder because of that."[13] Seb never explicitly articulates this point, but it seems impossible to imagine it does not inform his worldview. This fact of Seb's character—that he is aware of, but never explicitly articulates, his whiteness—is emblematic of *La La Land*'s racial representation as a whole: the film both ignores and draws attention to race. It is racially diverse on the surface, while ultimately reinscribing the white subjectivity of its leading couple, framing their white perspectives as normative.

The couple's whiteness sets *La La Land* apart from Chazelle's first film, *Guy and Madeline on a Park Bench*, which starred a non-white interracial couple (Jason Palmer, who is Black, and Desirée Garcia, who is Latina). According to Chazelle, when he was trying to get the movie made, he rewrote the character of Seb for each actor they offered the role to, some white and some Black.[14] Ultimately, Ryan Gosling's and Emma Stone's casting in the roles cemented the racial identities of the leading couple. *La La Land*'s cinematic world is racially diverse, but characters of color remain in the background or in supporting roles.

The focus on the white leading couple impacts the film's portrayal of jazz as a genre. As a narrative device, jazz remains a vehicle for the white characters to understand themselves.[15] Indeed, in the few diegetic jazz numbers in the film, Black musicians are consistently sidelined so that the focus remains on the white leading couple. When Seb takes Mia to the Lighthouse Café to show her what he finds so exciting about jazz, a combo consisting of older Black musicians plays a hard bop tune (Hurwitz's composition called "Herman's Habit"). Through a rapid montage, we see close-ups of the musicians' hands playing their instruments: first drums, then upright bass, then even more rapidly edited close-ups of all the instrumentalists' hands in quick succession, until the image cuts to a close-up of the trumpet player, flanked on either side by a saxophonist and a bassist, right on the downbeat of the head (Figure 4.1a). The trumpet obscures the musician's face, however, and as the camera zooms out, we see it only briefly before he recedes into the background with his bandmates (Figure 4.1b). The rest of the scene focuses on Mia and Seb, with the music and musicians remaining in the aural and visual background, despite the topic of their conversation. A brief cutaway from Mia and Seb reveals another rhythmic montage of the players' hands, but it is brief, and we rarely see their faces. Throughout, the musicians remain anonymous, almost faceless, more of a narrative device—an opportunity for Seb to explain his own understanding of the genre—than anything else.

(a)

(b)

Figures 4.1a–b "Herman's Habit," *La La Land*

A similar dynamic is at play in the "Summer Montage/Madeline" scene. This upbeat tune, repurposed from *Guy and Madeline*, plays over a montage of Mia and Seb's blossoming romance. The music, which fits a 1950s–1960s hard bop style, begins nondiegetically (Musical Example 4.1). Eventually, it becomes diegetically anchored when we see Seb playing piano with an otherwise all-Black combo at the Lighthouse Café. The other musicians are visible from the background, but Seb is highlighted through the use of a spotlight and camera framing (Figure 4.2a). We then see Mia dancing in the audience, surrounded by a group of onlookers who are all Black, and who seem genuinely entertained by her self-consciously awkward choreography (Figure 4.2b). The camera whip pans between Mia dancing and Seb playing a riff on the piano, in a kind of visual call-and-response pattern. Krin Gabbard suggests that the dynamic at play in this scene is a kind of "fantasy [that] is so typical of American jazz films in which black artists applaud and

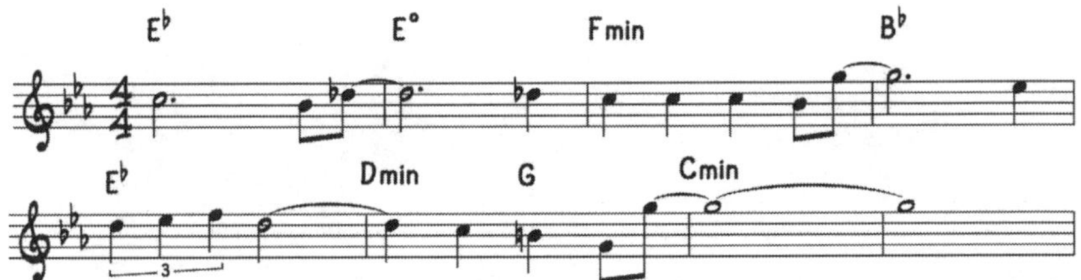

Musical Example 4.1 "Summer Montage/Madeline," excerpt (my transcription), *La La Land* (2016)

(a)

(b)

Figures 4.2a–b "Summer Montage/Madeline," *La La Land*

even congratulate white artists who have stolen their music."[16] This scene highlights a major tension in *La La Land*'s depiction of jazz: it shows an awareness of jazz's racial history, through the presence of Black musicians and audience members, but ultimately reinforces viewer identification with the white subjectivity of the lead characters.

This tension places *La La Land* in a long lineage of film musicals that sideline Black performers and appropriate Black performance styles. The contributions of Black musicians and dancers have substantially shaped the film musical since the genre's inception. As Todd Decker puts it, "as with virtually every kind of twentieth-century American popular music, the musical stage and screen has been intimately linked to African American musical styles; moreover, African Americans as a group have played defining roles as performers on the musical stage."[17] Performance of music by Black musicians was a common feature of Hollywood films, musical and otherwise, and Black characters onscreen were often depicted as musicians.[18] And throughout the history of the film musical, there have been high-profile films consisting of entirely Black casts.[19] In the mid-20th century, jazz was closely connected to Black performers in the film musical. One notable example is *Stormy Weather* (1943), a revue-style film that featured some of the most commercially successful Black talent of the day, including Lena Horne, Bill "Bojangles" Robinson, jazz bandleader and singer Cab Calloway, and jazz pianist Fats Waller. Films like *Stormy Weather* were important celebrations of Black talent onscreen, at the same time that Black performers' onscreen representation was restricted by white perceptions of Blackness.

Running just as deeply through the history of the film musical is the act of racial masquerading, or white performers appropriating Black styles of performance. The film musical was closely connected to blackface minstrelsy, a form of popular entertainment that dates back to the mid-19th century. Blackface minstrel performers would don dark makeup and imitate Black ways of walking, talking, singing, and dancing in a manner that relied on grotesque stereotypes but, despite its inaccuracy, was grounded in a discourse of authenticity.[20] Blackface performance outlived the minstrel tradition, becoming incorporated into vaudeville, musical theater, and film. The 1927 film *The Jazz Singer*, which is commonly understood to be the first widely distributed synchronized sound film and the first film musical, featured Al Jolson as a blackface singer, with several diegetic musical performances in blackface (a practice he was already known for on the stage). In this case, Jolson's blackface performance served to Americanize the Jewish immigrant character he portrayed.[21] Blackface performance was pervasive in Hollywood musicals through the 1940s, usually framed diegetically through a show-within-a-show conceit. The 1939 film *Babes in Arms*, for instance, featured Mickey Rooney and Judy Garland performing in blackface, depicting their embrace of the pervasive American tradition as cute.

Other films were less explicit in their racial masquerading. Many performers borrowed or drew from traditionally Black musical and choreographic styles without fully acknowledging their origins or influence. For instance, the early sound film *King of Jazz* (1930), a musical revue featuring songs all perceived as "jazz" at that time, starred white bandleader Paul Whiteman and his orchestra. Gabbard argues that "a more elaborate, more thorough denial of the African American role in jazz is difficult to imagine. . . . The repression of blackness leaves its mark all over the film: there are constant allusions to African Americans, and much of the film explicitly evokes minstrelsy, the film's grand predecessor in the ambivalent appropriation of blackness by whites."[22] The film's finale, titled "Melting Pot of Music," is a montage depicting various immigrant groups in costumes from their nation of origin, who all ostensibly become part of the American Melting Pot and contribute to the genre of jazz, but the number never once acknowledges Black musical culture. *King of Jazz* both reinforces and disavows its debt to Black musical performance, enacted with a cast of white performers.

Two of the most influential male dancers onscreen in the mid-20th century—Fred Astaire and Gene Kelly—also owed important debts to Black musical and choreographic traditions, but rarely credited these influences. (It is worth noting again that Astaire and Kelly were two big influences on *La La Land*, as discussed in Chapter 2.) Astaire clearly embodies the tensions and contradictions of racial masquerading in the film musical. Todd Decker has documented Astaire's close connection to Black styles of music and dance: he notes anecdotal accounts of Astaire's trips to Harlem to learn from Black dancers and points to the influence of jazz rhythms and musical structures on his style of choreography.[23] Although he rarely danced with Black dancers, Astaire would often perform while accompanied by Black musicians (for instance in the number "Slap That Bass" from *Shall We Dance* [1937]).[24] Decker suggests that Astaire's insistence on dancing to music made by Black musicians was marked "by explicit racial boundary crossing."[25] Astaire performed in blackface onscreen only once—the "Bojangles of Harlem" number in *Swing Time* (1936)—but other numbers he performed were more implicitly racialized, such as "Steppin' Out with My Baby" from *Easter Parade* (1948). It is clear that Astaire's relationship to Black musical and dance styles permeates his career. Without denying their influence, he nevertheless often depicted them in ways his audiences perceived as racially unmarked (i.e., "white").

Similarly, Kelly's dance style owed debts to Black performers, but that debt is rarely acknowledged. His choreography in the "Chocolat" section of his *American in Paris* (1951) ballet exemplifies Kelly's approach to race in his choreography: although he did not use blackface, it is nevertheless an extremely racialized sequence in its use of gesture, costume, and music. On a broader scale, *Singin' in the Rain* (1952) is a particularly apt example of the racial appropriation that often occurred in less explicit, more insidious ways in the Hollywood musical. Carol Clover suggests that the choreography in *Singin' in the Rain* exemplifies an "anxiety of influence," bringing up but then negating in different ways the influence of Black dancers and dance styles: "What *Singin' in the Rain* doesn't-but-does know is that the real art of the film musical is dance, that a crucial talent source for that art is African-American performance, and that, relative to its contribution, this talent source is undercredited and underpaid."[26] Both Gene Kelly and co-star Donald O'Connor took pride in being "accepted and appreciated" by Black performers.[27] But a film like *Singin' in the Rain* disavows this indebtedness.

As these examples attest, *La La Land*'s approach to jazz through a white frame can be understood as participating in a long trend that runs through the history of the film musical, where white performers sideline the artistic contributions of Black musicians. Seb's crusade to "save" jazz is thus another example of erasure of Black contributions to American popular music and to the film musical more broadly.

With this context in mind, Seb's project to "save" jazz becomes particularly problematic. It turns *La La Land*, according to Ira Madison III, into "a Trojan horse white-savior film."[28] As Madison suggests, "If you're gonna make a film about an artist staying true to the roots of jazz against the odds and against modern reinventions of the genre . . . you'd think that artist would be black." Whom, exactly, is Seb saving jazz from? And who is he to decide that jazz needs saving in the first place? Although he idolizes Black musicians like John Coltrane, Louis Armstrong, and Thelonious Monk, he never once really listens to the perspective of the Black musicians he plays with. This mentality is not a healthy one for the future of jazz: as David A. Graham suggests, "A music based in black popular culture and shaped over the years by black musicians—with significant but on balance lesser contributions from whites—is unlikely to thrive as an artistic or commercial realm if it shrinks to become the province of white, middle-class men who went to conservatories to learn to play blues scales playing concerts attended by white, middle-class men."[29] And although a Black man—Keith—warns him of the perils of his narrow viewpoint of jazz, Seb is unwilling to listen.

Sebastian as Sellout?: *La La Land*, Keith, and the Debate over Fusion

In Sebastian's resistance to "selling out," Keith is his major foil. Keith is a music school friend of Seb's who has attained success with his band the Messengers and invites Seb to play keyboards with the band for a national tour. The Messengers play jazz-inflected popular music, and Keith has clearly embraced popular styles without any qualms. To Sebastian, Keith's success—and, by extension, his own involvement with the Messengers—is directly at odds with the stylistic purity he himself values most highly. By achieving fame and fortune, Keith has sold out, and Sebastian feels he has done the same by joining the band.

The casting of John Legend as Keith adds further dimension to the film's portrayal of the polarity of selling out versus stylistic purity, folding Legend's biography into the audience's understanding of the character. Legend, born John Roger Stephens, is a Grammy-winning singer, songwriter, pianist, and producer. Influenced by gospel and soul growing up, he began playing piano at a young age, performed in musicals while in high school, and directed a jazz-pop a cappella group in college. He began his career collaborating with other famous musicians, including Lauryn Hill and Kanye West, and in 2004 his debut album *Get Lifted* was a critical and commercial hit, going gold and winning him a Grammy for Best R&B Album.[30] Legend went on to collaborate with a range of musicians and release numerous solo albums, and he is the first Black musician to win the EGOT (Emmy, Grammy, Oscar, and Tony Awards).

Legend first met with Chazelle in his capacity as a producer. Chazelle asked if Legend was interested in executive producing, as well as providing music for Keith and the Messengers. But he eventually asked him if he wanted to play Keith; according to Legend, "the character had some similarities to my own background as a musician. Damien thought I could relate to the character, and I felt the same way."[31] *La La Land* was Legend's first acting role; to prepare for the part, he worked with an acting coach and learned to play guitar.[32] According to Chazelle, the Keith character changed across different drafts of the script. There were times he felt "too simplistically antagonistic" and other times he felt "so similar to Sebastian, in a way, that the conflict wasn't exactly clear."[33] Chazelle needed someone who could strike the balance, who could "thread the needle."[34] Legend resonated with Chazelle because of his classical training and subsequent mainstream success. Chazelle wanted to cast a real musician who could "bring an authenticity to the part that would keep it from just being a simple plot device," while also bringing enough "presence, charisma, charm, and weight to persuade Sebastian to do something that goes against his own impulses," and he felt that Legend had both "this kind of slick charisma and a warm humanity."[35]

Though Legend's career is accomplished and extensive, and though he was broadly musically trained, his music is rarely, if ever, considered jazz fusion, or even explicitly influenced by jazz. Legend himself has claimed that he does not consider himself "much of a jazz aficionado," and although he grew up listening to classic jazz vocalists like Ella Fitzgerald and Billie Holiday, the genre was not a strong influence on his musical development.[36] As a result, the debate becomes more about the implications of catering to popular tastes in general than about the specific contemporary aesthetics or cultural position of jazz fusion.

As a foil to Seb's staunch traditionalism, Keith is an important figure in the film. Chazelle claims that we are not supposed to side with either Seb or Keith, but to understand both sides.[37] Keith's monologue during Seb's first rehearsal with the Messengers, where Seb clearly harbors doubts about his decision to play with the band, sums up Keith's side of the debate succinctly. He says to Seb, "You say you wanna save jazz. How are you gonna save jazz if no one's listening? Jazz is dying because of people like you. . . . How are you gonna be a revolutionary if you're such a traditionalist? You're holding on to the past, but jazz is about the future." This sentiment is difficult to refute, especially since many of the jazz legends Seb reveres were revolutionaries during their time. Seb, in other words, is supposed to be seen as a stick-in-the-mud. Chazelle claimed to me that he believes that Keith is "pretty much right": "I tend to side with Keith in that conversation, even though emotionally, obviously, I have a lot of sympathy for Sebastian's position."[38] But Chazelle's emotional sympathy for Sebastian's perspective pervades the film in different ways. Perhaps Gosling's charismatic performance makes Seb more likable than he was intended, therefore eliciting greater audience identification with his perspective than with Keith's.

For Legend's part, he claims that he did not consider the film's racial representation while making it, but he nevertheless acknowledged after the fact that the film should not be understood as representative of jazz:

> I guess a lot of times pressure is put on something after it becomes big. Because it ends up being *the* jazz film. But when you're just making it, it's Damien's point of view. He's a filmmaker. He's the screenwriter, he's the director, and he's telling a story from his own point of view. If you want the film to represent all things jazz, it does not. . . . But, if you just see it as one guy's point of view, one filmmaker's point of view, and one story among many stories that can be told about jazz, then it's not as much of an issue. . . .
>
> If you were trying to make a film about what jazz is and its origins and who plays it now, then of course there should be a lot of black people. Black people invented jazz. But this story wasn't ever claiming to be that. It's just a story about two people from one writer's point of view.[39]

Although by all accounts Legend had a lot of agency in shaping Keith's character—he improvised his monologue, for instance—it was all within the broader framework of the film's existing narrative.

Additionally, through its music, the film seems to implicitly favor Seb's perspective over Keith's. The only glimpse into Keith's "viable alternative" to Seb's traditionalism is in the Messengers' song "Start a Fire," which, through lyrics, production style, and visual framing, is depicted as an overly commercial aesthetic compromise. The song was a collaboration between Hurwitz, Marius de Vries, Legend, and Angelique Cinelu, a songwriter and sometimes-collaborator with Legend. Chazelle claimed the song needed to walk a fine line between "being very distinctively different from the rest of the musical material in the film, but also at the same time being . . . a good piece of music."[40] Legend said of the song:

> The main instruction was make it a fun song that you can see as a single that still has some jazz influence, but could tell it was leaning in more of a pop direction than most music you would call jazz. It had to feel like it was still good and a viable alternative, but Sebastian would feel like it was selling out a bit. It was having to thread the needle because you don't want it to be so bad that it's embarrassing, but you want it to be something that Sebastian wouldn't want to make. Something he wouldn't be proud of.[41]

In other words, it had to be catchy and believably good enough that Seb would willingly accept the gig, but commercially "tainted" enough that it was clear Seb was selling out by playing it.

As Hurwitz describes it, writing the song was a collaborative process: Legend developed the idea for the initial melody, Hurwitz primarily devised the chord changes, Hurwitz and Legend together came up with the rest of the melodic material, de Vries worked on a drum groove, and Cinelu and Legend wrote most of the lyrics. The original version that came out of that session, according to Hurwitz, was almost entirely in minor, was "more R&B," and "was actually much cooler" than the final version. In order to give it a poppier sensibility, Hurwitz later reharmonized the melody, replacing B-flat minor with B-flat major chords to add "brightness" at the beginning of the song. He also added the fizzy synthesizer sounds to make it "cheesier and cheesier."[42] The result is something that starkly contrasts with the rest of the numbers in the film.

"Start a Fire" is the sole performance of the Messengers in the film. The scene begins in darkness. We hear the cheers of a large crowd, then a minor chord on the piano, as a spotlight illuminates Seb playing on the stage. He begins playing a rubato riff on the piano that sounds like "traditional" jazz that he might typically play. As he arpeggiates a half cadence, he looks out at the crowd in a medium close-up and smiles slightly at Mia, who smiles back from the crowd in a reaction shot (Figures 4.3a–b). Then, the camera cuts back to the stage as a new spotlight illuminates Keith, who sings, "I don't know why I keep moving my body," to a simple piano accompaniment. But as the first phrase of the song concludes, the second one begins in full force: the lights come up on the stage to reveal a whole band, including electric guitar and backup singers, illuminated by the band's name in bright lights behind them, as Seb turns to his synthesizer and begins to play more pop-infused accompaniment (Figure 4.3c–d). We see Mia's reaction, which is one of confusion and perhaps a bit of condescension (Figure 4.3e). She begins to groove slightly to the song, attempting to embrace its catchiness, as we see Seb's forced expressions of enjoyment. By the chorus, all seems to have reached an acceptable musical compromise, despite the generic, cheesy lyrics: "Don't you know I feel so good tonight." But as the second verse begins, dancers enter the stage and begin performing energetic, modern, sexualized choreography that is very obviously from the commercial, popular music realm. At this point, we see Mia's confused reaction. Seb's smile is completely artificial, as he barely masks his displeasure (Figure 4.3f). During the synthesizer solo

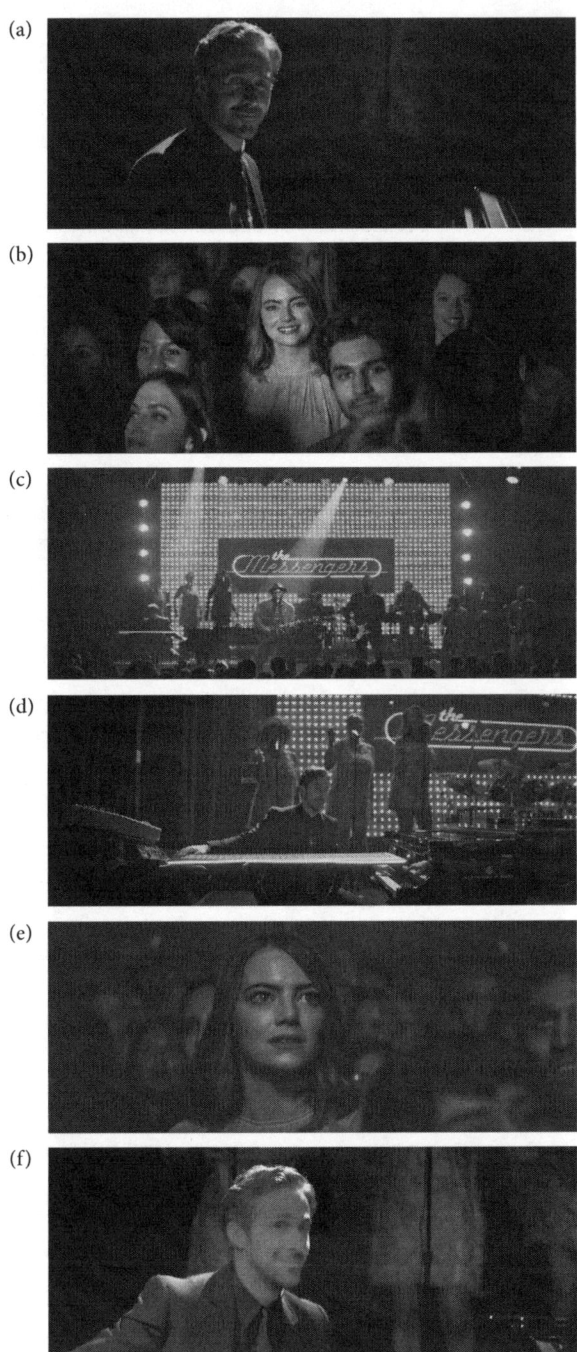

Figures 4.3a–f "Start a Fire," *La La Land*

that follows, Mia gets pushed further and further back in the crowd. The crowd loves the music, but Mia is clearly flummoxed as to why Seb would agree to play something that he so obviously stands against.

Ultimately, the number is a catchy pop song that stands in stark contrast with the rest of the score. Though on the surface *La La Land* may be presenting both Seb's and Keith's approaches to jazz as equally viable options, Mia and Seb's disdain for what Keith represents is obvious in this scene, and by extension, the viewer is supposed to find this musical performance too commercial, too cheesy, straying too far from "real" jazz. Seve Chambers suggests that with Keith's "laughably '80s sound that's meant to seem completely disconnected from his jazz roots" and his "cheesy stage show complete with dancers," Chazelle "stacks the deck against" Keith and his perspective about innovating.[43] Mandy Moore choreographed the onstage dance for the number. She claims that, as "commercial dance," it was "a lot closer to my lane" than the choreography for the other songs, and although she was insistent that the scene not "come across as a parody," the choreography pokes fun at the presence of sexualized dancers on pop stars' concert stages.[44] Though the diegetic crowd goes wild, Seb makes a face that betrays his embarrassment at playing this style of music. The close-up of Mia's face says it all: as the film's audience, we are meant to understand that this commercially successful style of music is a form of "selling out," not the "pure" jazz Sebastian wants to play. That Keith is the only character of color with a substantial role in the film, and that he seems to make artistic compromises that are shown as in poor taste, only serves to reinforce the white savior trope.

La La Land's Missing L.A. Jazz Narrative

The film ends with a glimpse into Seb's nightclub five years later. Per Mia's earlier suggestion, he has foregone the esoteric name "Chicken on a Stick" in favor of the more concise (and broadly inviting) "Seb's." But otherwise, he seems to have made zero compromises to his artistic integrity in order to achieve success. Mia and her husband wander in off the street after hearing music wafting from the basement. Seb's is pristine, upscale, and elite. The musicians onstage are almost all Black, but the audience is racially mixed. Instead of dancing, like Mia did at the Lighthouse Café earlier in the film, the audience sits and politely listens, a sign of the genre's respectability. The success of Seb's seems to implicitly reinforce Sebastian's narrow definition of "pure" jazz, as a rarefied thing of the past, and to suggest that it still has a place in today's world.

With the diegetic settings for jazz performance limited to the Lighthouse Café and Seb's, a viewer of *La La Land* unaware of contemporary jazz would never know that there was in fact a rich L.A.-based jazz scene in the years immediately preceding the film, a scene that sounds nothing like either the rarefied neo-bop that Seb plays or the 1980s-synth-infused, jazz-inflected pop of the Messengers. A collective of musicians known as the West Coast Get Down (WCGD), which includes saxophonist Kamasi Washington and bassist Stephen Bruner (better known as Thundercat), exploded on the scene in the 2010s, owing to their fusion of jazz with elements of funk, soul, and hip-hop.[45] They were catapulted to mainstream success when they collaborated with rapper Kendrick Lamar on his widely acclaimed *To Pimp a Butterfly* (2015), a hip-hop album that is thoroughly steeped in jazz performance. The experimental electronic-jazz musician and producer Flying Lotus, who has closely collaborated with members of WCGD, also got his start in L.A. Many of these L.A.-based musicians are children of accomplished jazz musicians who were active in the 1960s and 1970s, and they developed their musical voices in the context of the harsh conditions of their predominantly Black neighborhoods at a time when Los Angeles was a center of West Coast rap. Blending hip-hop sensibilities with jazz, these musicians draw young crowds who, in the words of WCGD trombonist Ryan Porter, "mov[e] their bodies like it's a rock concert. . . . They can see that our music is about taking people's perceptions of jazz and flipping them upside down."[46] Playing at L.A.'s Club Nokia (later renamed Novo), these musicians have been credited with redefining jazz for a new generation of listeners, many of whom approach the genre through the point of entry of hip-hop, electronic music, or soul. Each member of the WCGD collective aims "to push jazz to the forefront of culture, just like it was in the 1950s."[47] Some critics suggest that the L.A. jazz scene has created a jazz renaissance, or a new "golden age" for the genre.[48]

Even outside of L.A., there are many influential musicians today who push the boundaries of the jazz genre, like Esperanza Spalding, Robert Glasper, and Vijay Iyer, redefining contemporary notions of what jazz sounds like and who it is for. According to Greg Tate, this revival in the world of jazz "refuse[s] any opposition between software-driven sonic modernity and a good old-fashioned bebop-infested blowing session—both in the studio or on the stage."[49] Though these fusion musicians blend traditional jazz with a range of genres and styles, some of them popular, it would be inaccurate to characterize them as "sellouts": they are frequently lauded as innovators for their experimental musical approaches. Moreover, the arc of their careers and the audiences their concerts draw are very different from *La La Land*'s representation of jazz fusion through Keith and the Messengers.

The contemporary L.A. jazz scene, embodied in the musicians of the WCGD collective, Flying Lotus, and others, reveals that in reality there is an alternative to the either/or, purist or sellout narrative of *La La Land*. Indeed, there was energetic experimentalism taking place in the jazz world within Seb and Mia's city at the very time they wandered through L.A. as a couple; they just were not looking (or listening) in the right places. These contemporary jazz musicians were effortlessly blending their influences, innovating jazz in a manner that has also brought them critical acclaim. That Seb is unaware of these trends, or perhaps unwilling to acknowledge them, further entrenches the whiteness of *La La Land*'s jazz narrative and the way in which the film's nostalgia is racialized.

La La Land's Jazz Ambivalence

Mia and Sebastian's romance is musically represented through a leitmotif that recurs throughout the film, aptly titled "Mia & Sebastian's Theme." It's a simple waltz with a two-bar rhythmic motive. The theme bookends the couple's relationship: Sebastian plays it in the restaurant when they first lock eyes, and again in his jazz club when they see each other, years later, from across the room (Musical Example 4.2). "Mia & Sebastian's Theme" becomes a flight of fancy that highlights the fantastical nature of their relationship. In its wistful melancholy, it embodies the film's nostalgia. But diegetically, it requires suspension of disbelief to imagine it as a theme that Sebastian would have written; it certainly does not fit into the narrowly defined "jazz" style he typically plays. The melody is too linear, too rubato, and the harmonization underneath barely contains any jazz voicing; it is much more indebted to European musical styles than American ones, a stylistic debt that the film seems to disavow. The only time we hear this song with any hint of his preferred neo-bop style is the first time he plays it in the restaurant: here, his performance culminates in a jazz-inflected cadenza, a cynical musical flourish to the action Seb knows has cost him his job. Perhaps more importantly,

Musical Example 4.2 Mia & Sebastian's Theme (excerpt), *La La Land* (2016)

Mia & Sebastian's Theme
from LA LA LAND
Music by Justin Hurwitz
© 2016 B Lion Music (BMI) administered by Songs Of Universal, Inc. (BMI)/Warner-Tamerlane
    Publishing Corp. (BMI)
This arrangement © 2023 B Lion Music (BMI) administered by Songs Of Universal, Inc.
    (BMI)/Warner-Tamerlane Publishing Corp. (BMI)
All Rights Reserved   Used by Permission
Reprinted by permission of Hal Leonard LLC

though "Mia & Sebastian's Theme" is stylistically mismatched with Seb's musical sensibilities, its nostalgia connects more broadly to Seb's own nostalgia for an era of jazz that he never experienced first-hand.

La La Land's jazz narrative is complex and multivalent. It celebrates jazz, but in the narrowest possible terms. Through the character of Keith, it critiques Seb's hardheaded nostalgia and unwillingness to look to the future, but ultimately, Seb's mentality is upheld and even celebrated. It subtly acknowledges the genre's racial origins while at the same time disavowing or ignoring them. Ultimately, the tensions at play in *La La Land's* jazz narrative are symbolic of the film's tensions as a whole. It critiques nostalgia, while simultaneously embracing it; establishes a diverse, multiracial world, while ultimately reinscribing the white experience of its leading couple; and reinvents the film musical for the 21st century, while drawing on mid-20th-century aesthetics and tropes to do so. Its portrayal of jazz, therefore, serves as a microcosm of the film.

5

Reception

A *Saturday Night Live* sketch on January 21, 2017, begins with host Aziz Ansari sitting in an interrogation room.[1] Two detectives (played by Cecily Strong and Beck Bennett) walk into the room. Ansari has no idea why he has been arrested. What comes next sounds like it could be straight out of a crime drama: "Shut up, punk. You know what you did." "I can't even look at you. You disgust me." "Last night. Seven p.m. Ring any bells?" Then comes the twist. His crime? He didn't love *La La Land.* The cops show him security footage from a restaurant where he admits to a woman he is dating that "it was good, but I thought it kind of dragged in the middle" (Figure 5.1). They call him a "sick son-of-a-bitch" before proclaiming that "*La La Land* is a perfect film." Ansari defends himself with soft critiques of the film, which the cops proceed to rebut: "I liked it, I just thought there were too many montages in the middle." "That's how you show the passage of time, you dumb mother—." "I guess I just didn't think it was, like, *amazing* singing." "That's the effing point!" "It's a whole movie about jazz and there's no Black people in it!" "I didn't realize John Legend was white. . . . I didn't realize that couple on the bridge was also white." At one point, they ask him, "What do you like if you don't like *La La Land*?" and he replies, "I dunno, I guess *Moonlight*?" They pause their interrogation to briefly agree on *Moonlight*'s importance, only to admit they have not yet seen it.

The *SNL* sketch humorously encapsulated the evolving reception of *La La Land*: the film's initial near-unanimous critical praise was followed by a backlash in some quarters, reflecting the polarizing nature of its approach to reviving and contemporizing the film musical genre. The sketch playfully pokes fun at the hyperbolic praise used by many fans of *La La Land*, while also pointing to some of the critiques leveraged against the film. The polarized reactions became such a pervasive part of its image in popular culture that a *New York Times* article appeared in February titled "Love *La La Land*? Hate It? So Do We."[2]

This chapter examines *La La Land*'s reception, from its initial film festival run in the summer of 2016 through the Academy Awards ceremony in

Figure 5.1 Saturday Night Live *La La Land* Interrogation Sketch, January 2017

February 2017. The backlash that emerged in the fall of 2016 can in part be understood as a typical response to a film that initially garners such effusive praise early in its run. But its evolving reception was shaped by several additional factors. A shift in national mood in response to current events right around its premiere (mainly the 2016 presidential election) impacted views of the film as either a much-needed diversion from reality or a problematic dive into backward-looking nostalgia. Additionally, *La La Land*'s reception was profoundly shaped by the simultaneous critical success of *Moonlight*, a much lower-budget film about a queer Black man that in many ways seemed to symbolize everything *La La Land* lacked in terms of diversity and representation. The two films have since become intertwined in cultural memory, owing to the spectacular Best Picture mix-up at the Oscars, which, though an accident, has impacted *La La Land*'s reception since. Though Hollywood has long had a reputation as politically liberal, it has often reinscribed well-worn stereotypes and excluded different kinds of stories from being told, less out of malice than out of ignorance, owing to the overwhelming homogeneity of writers and executives (straight white men). The debates around *La La Land*—as a film that seemed to uncritically reinscribe whiteness through its narrative and casting choices—captured the essence of much broader cultural debates that were taking place around Hollywood, representation, and the kinds of stories and experiences that were being valued and presented onscreen.

Praise for *La La Land*

La La Land premiered at the Venice Film Festival in August 2016 to nearly unanimous critical praise from mainstream outlets.[3] According to accounts of the festival, the film "swept critics right off their feet,"[4] leaving them "stunned"[5] and "breathless."[6] Indeed, at the opening press screening, critics burst into applause at the end of the opening number, "Another Day of Sun," and warmly applauded at the end of the film, a rare occurrence for the Venice festival.[7] Critics were captivated by the film's blend of nostalgia and contemporary novelty in its approach to updating the classic Hollywood musical. For instance, Todd McCarthy of *The Hollywood Reporter* praised it as "utterly unexpected and original," writing that "lovers of classic musicals will be swept away" by "a welcome gift of vintage goods in a dazzling new package."[8] Many commented on what they considered Chazelle's daring approach to audiovisual style and cinematic form: Owen Gleiberman of *Variety* called it "the most audacious big-screen musical in a long time,"[9] and McCarthy suggested that "for Chazelle to be able to pull this off the way he has is something close to remarkable."[10] Pete Hammond of *Deadline* noted that no film in a long time had been "quite this lyrical, lovely, and most importantly, *original* on the screen."[11]

Critics particularly responded to what they saw as an earnest embrace of the film musical genre, without cynicism or parody. Gleiberman wrote:

A lot of people still find old musicals corny or think (mistakenly) that they're quaint. Yet the form remains stubbornly alive in the bones of our culture. That's why it feels so right, in "La La Land," to see a daring filmmaker go whole hog in re-creating a lavish studio-system musical, replete with starry nights and street lamps lighting up the innocence of soft-shoe romance, and two people who were meant for each other literally dancing on air.[12]

Stephanie Zacharek of *Time* agreed, calling *La La Land* a "glorious, openhearted musical."[13] Similarly, critics labeled it a feel-good movie, despite the bittersweet ending: Peter Bradshaw of the *Guardian* called it a "happy, sweet-natured movie—something to give you a vitamin-D boost of sunshine,"[14] and Hammond wrote that "this is a movie worth savoring, something that entertains, enlightens and makes us feel good about being alive."[15] Critics also singled out the performances of the leading couple, praising Emma

Stone and Ryan Gosling as "incredible actors and singers,"[16] "a modern answer to Fred Astaire and Cyd Charisse," and "a duo . . . close to perfection."[17] Stone's performance was particularly lauded, and she won the Volpi Cup for Best Actress. The film's reception at Venice cleared the way to make it an "instant Oscar front-runner on its way to becoming a classic of the genre."[18] The European cinephile contingency of the Venice audience was in many ways predisposed to respond positively to *La La Land*'s aesthetic, particularly as a spiritual successor to the films of Jacques Demy. Moreover, self-reflexive films often play well with film industry insiders, and *La La Land* was doubly so: both a movie about the movies and one rife with intertextual references to classic films. No matter the reason, *La La Land*'s rave reception at Venice had a profound impact on how it was subsequently received in North America.

The momentum of *La La Land*'s success at Venice continued in September at the Telluride Film Festival in Colorado. The film was given a coveted place on the program: the Friday afternoon Patron Preview slot. The packed audience gave two standing ovations in the middle of the film—one after "Another Day of Sun" and another after the Observatory scene.[19] Later in the festival, actor Tom Hanks interrupted a Q&A for his film *Sully* to praise *La La Land* and urge everyone to see it.[20] Critical praise for the film echoed that coming out of Venice: the "intricate, wondrously executed modern musical" was "technically dazzling"[21] and "a lavish and lovely musical romance."[22] A couple weeks later at the Toronto International Film Festival, after receiving yet another standing ovation, *La La Land* won the audience award for Best Feature Film, an award that is often thought to predict success at the Oscars.[23] According to *Los Angeles Times* reporter Steven Zeitchik, it received "one of the strongest responses in recent TIFF memory."[24] *Vulture* critic Jada Yuan described how, in front of a mostly American and Canadian audience, "its charm proved undeniable, likely to audiences and Academy members alike, as the kind of pure-of-heart crowd-pleaser that rarely, if ever, gets made anymore."[25]

La La Land continued on the festival circuit, playing at the BFI London Film Festival in early October, Middleburg Film Festival in late October, and the Virginia Film Festival and AFI Fest in November. It continued to be featured as the centerpiece film, garnering praise and winning awards (such as the Virginia Film Festival's grand prize).[26] In many respects, its success with film festival audiences is not surprising; as one critic suggested in considering its prospects at the Oscars, the film was "almost tailor-made for Academy members."[27] The critical acclaim from Venice had a snowball effect, increasing Oscar buzz that in turn generated more interest. By the time it was released to general audiences in December, the movie had already cemented its reputation as one of the best films of 2016 and a possible contender for the Academy Award for Best Picture. Critics latched onto its mixture of nostalgia and contemporary sensibilities; many reminisced about an older era of filmmaking, suggesting that Chazelle had tapped into the style of classic Hollywood while modernizing the film musical at the same time. A. O. Scott of the *New York Times* predicted that the "mixture of antiquarian precision and entrepreneurial self-confidence that drives 'La La Land' will be embraced by a generation for whom preservation and invention often go together."[28]

La La Land premiered to general audiences on December 9, 2016, expanding to additional cities on December 16, and critics continued to rave about it. By this time, however, the national mood had shifted considerably, owing to the election of Donald Trump as president. The victory of this polarizing figure took much of the country by surprise, especially those living in blue states. For many white coastal-elite liberals, including in the film industry, Trump's election was a wake-up call that racist, misogynistic, and anti-immigrant mentalities continued to resonate for many Americans. (Marginalized groups, of course, had no such luxury to believe that these mentalities had been left in the past.) As a result of this shift in national mood, *La La Land* reached the general public at a very different cultural moment. Some saw it as a welcome distraction from current events; for instance, *New York Times* critic Manohla Dargis articulated the difference in her experiences watching the film before and after the election:

> The first time I watched Damien Chazelle's musical, "La La Land," I thought a lot about how it worked, about its form, his craft and how the lickable candy-colored costumes bring to mind both M&M's and Jacques Demy. I thought about how Mr. Chazelle and his stars, Emma Stone and Ryan Gosling, fit into the history of the film musical. When I went to see "La La Land" again, I was in a terrible state, and this time I just fell into it, gratefully. I surrendered. Afterward, I realized that this must have been what it was like to watch Fred Astaire and Ginger Rogers during the Great Depression.[29]

Although most did not explicitly point to the election aftermath in their assessment of the film, other critics echoed a similar desire to escape into its nostalgia: Anthony Lane of the *New Yorker* said that the film's "idea—that nostalgia can be gutsy and purposeful rather than moony and limp—is what powers 'La La Land,'"[30] and for Brian Truitt of *USA Today*, it was "life-affirming food for the soul."[31] Mick LaSalle of *SF Gate* described it as "a beautiful and hopeful film, coming at a time when there isn't much beauty or hope in our movies,"[32] and in the *Seattle Times*, Moira Macdonald called it "a gift from the movie gods . . . right when a lot of us are in desperate need of some light."[33] Critics responded anew to the feel-good elements, this time with an urgency that had not been present in the months prior. Interestingly, the poignant ending did not seem to dampen the film's ability to function as diversionary entertainment for critics.

Even when not directly commenting on the film as distraction from contemporary politics, many reviewers pointed out the contemporary, 21st-century sensibilities of *La La Land.* According to critics, the film was "a tribute to an era where musicals and jazz ruled but also posit[ed] in powerful fashion how each needs to evolve for its own relevance";[34] it embraced "the present while paying tribute to the past, by balancing irony and innocence, novelty and nostalgia";[35] and it told "a modern story about modern people, and just in passing assures audiences that today can be just as magical as the past, that we modern people are worth a musical, too," doing so in a manner that was "fresh and vital."[36] Again, the blend of nostalgia and novelty was seen as one of the film's biggest contributions, proposed as a path forward for the future of the film musical genre.

La La Land continued to gain accolades—the New York Film Critics Circle named it the best film of 2016, and the Critics' Choice Awards nominated the film twelve times. It was nominated for seven Golden Globe awards and won each one (including Best Motion Picture—Musical or Comedy, Best Director, Best Actor—Comedy or Musical, and Best Actress—Comedy or Musical), breaking previous records. It also garnered tremendous box office success, grossing $151.1 million in the United States and Canada, and $446.1 million worldwide.[37] The film was well on its way to entering the pantheon of Hollywood classics.

Critiques and Backlash

When a film, or any cultural phenomenon, receives as many accolades as *La La Land* did in the first months of its run, it is natural for critics and fans to respond by tempering that praise, viewing initial reactions as perhaps over-blown or overhyped. This was certainly the case with *La La Land*, but to an exceptional degree. Indeed, by the beginning of 2017, although the accolades continued, the ongoing critical response to *La La Land* had become decidedly more mixed. As Emily Yahr points out in a January article for the *Washington Post* titled "Your Guide to the 'La La Land' Backlash," it is difficult "to pinpoint when the narrative changed from 'Oh, you *must* see "La La Land"' to 'Well, "La La Land" wasn't *that* great.' But it seems that as more people see the movie . . . public opinion is tilting toward the latter."[38] At the same time that the film continued to rack up awards and nominations, public sentiment around it began to shift. For some, it was a general feeling that *La La Land* was not good enough to usher in a resurgence of the Hollywood musical the way many claimed it would. In other words, it was a fine film, but not worthy of the kind of hyperbolic praise it was receiving. But as *La La Land* moved into widespread release, it experienced a more profound backlash that solidified around several key critiques of aspects seen as either overlooked or misunderstood by earlier critical assessments.

Some of these critiques were around the very aesthetic choices that had resonated so deeply for so many upon its initial release. For instance, whereas the leading couple's lack of singing and dance training was endearing to many, others began to criticize this choice, believing that the film suffered as a result. Kelly Lawler wrote in *USA Today* that "Oscar nominees Gosling and Stone, while great actors, are also simply not truly trained singers, and their thin vocals are evident throughout the film."[39] Morgan Leigh Davies, in the *Los Angeles Review of Books*, expressed the same sentiment, further suggesting that this lack of skill called into question the film's status as a musical:

> Emma Stone and Ryan Gosling are charming presences, but they are not accomplished singers, and Stone can't dance. One wonders, then: Why were they cast in the first place? The practical explanation is obvious—they are movie stars—but in that case, why is *La La Land* a musical at all? Most of the story is told outside of its musical numbers, which are peppered in to add flavor but don't drive the engine of the plot.[40]

Robin Pogrebin of the *New York Times* concurred: "Yes, better a new Hollywood musical than no new Hollywood musical. But the high hopes raised by the inventive opening number are dashed by the weak delivery of its stars. Let's face it, they can't really sing or dance. And the novelty of seeing celebrities try to pull it off wears thin pretty fast."[41] In the *Observer*, Rex Reed was even more pointed in his critique: "Ryan Gosling can't sing and Emma Stone is no Cyd Charisse. When he croons a love song, he's so flat and out of tune it made me wince. His dancing is better but rudimentary, which is surprising considering his early years in the Mickey Mouse Club. Together their charisma wouldn't fill a demitasse."[42] Where earlier critics had praised the leading actors' performances, viewing their amateur singing and dancing as part of what made their characters relatable, others saw the casting of movie stars rather than triple threats in the leading roles as a missed opportunity to showcase truly impressive musical and choreographic talent in a genre purported to care about such things.

Additionally, the intertextual references to classic Hollywood films, considered one of the film's great strengths by many, began to be viewed by others as unoriginal recycling of content, or worse. Rex Reed wrote that *La La Land* "reeks of mothballs," suggesting that it "comes off as a well-intended tribute to the fabulous MGM musicals of the great Vincente Minnelli, made by people who have never seen one."[43] For some critics, *La La Land*'s references were more than a boring aesthetic choice: the intertextuality bought into a problematic form of nostalgia, related to the very nostalgia that had led to the ascendency of President Trump's slogan "Make America Great Again," and audiences' embrace of this nostalgia was similarly troubling. (The title of Manohla Dargis's *New York Times* review even echoed the slogan, however unintentionally, when it claimed the film "Makes Musicals Matter Again."[44]) In his article "The Unbearable Whiteness of *La La Land*," Geoff Nelson reminded readers of the dangers of nostalgia for a pre–Civil Rights era, cuttingly arguing that "the film . . . functions as an ode to a lost era of white supremacy, and its viewers, consciously or unconsciously, participate in the delusion. The film's politics of nostalgia and whiteness are inextricable."[45]

Indeed, the most significant critiques leveraged against the film had to do with its whiteness; its representation of race, particularly through its jazz narrative; and its gender politics, which many saw as regressive and anything but contemporary. Simply put, for many viewers, *La La Land* reinscribed the classic Hollywood musical's whiteness through its leading couple, relegating actors of color to the margins. Ty Burr of the *Boston Globe*, for instance, wrote of its "unfortunate reliance on people of color as accent notes of authenticity in a white romantic playground."[46]

Critics frequently wrote about the jazz narrative as a particularly troubling aspect of the film. Former basketball player Kareem Abdul-Jabbar wrote an opinion piece for the *Hollywood Reporter*, suggesting that although he found the film "bold, daring and deserving of all its critical and financial success," its representation of race and jazz was worth interrogating:

> No, I don't think the film needs more black people. Writer-director Damien Chazelle should tell the story as he sees fit with whatever ethnic arrangement he desires. However, it is fair to question his color wheel when it involves certain historical elements—such as jazz. The white guy wants to preserve the black roots of jazz while the black guy is the sellout? This could be a deliberate ironic twist, but if it is, it's a distasteful one for African-Americans.[47]

Writing in *Wired*, Ruby Lott-Lavigna suggested that the jazz narrative made the film "dated by its racial politics":

> It focuses on jazz while seemingly pushing the black Americans who pioneered the genre into the background. We constantly hear Gosling explaining how he will save jazz, while behind him black men play the music *they* created. It's patronising at times, with scenes showing Gosling playing jazz piano as the only focal point of the camera, or Stone dancing to jazz, both outlined by people of colour, footnotes in a representation of their culture. Various musicians have come out to critique the lack of black or queer characters in a film about jazz and musicals, and it's a frustrating watch in 2016.[48]

Alison Willmore of *BuzzFeed* wrote, "It's a privilege of whiteness to feel such an unabashed sense of ownership over a genre of music as fundamentally grounded in the black experience as jazz the way Sebastian does."[49] The jazz narrative tapped into a long history of racial masquerading in the Hollywood musical, as I detailed in Chapter 4, which was especially provocative at a time when the lack of diverse representation in Hollywood was increasingly becoming a topic of cultural conversation.

Critics pointed out the ways in which the jazz narrative was gendered as well. Anna Silman claimed that "no director has done more for the image of the Male Music Nerd in popular culture than Damien Chazelle," and that Chazelle "wants us to love not just jazz, but also to love men who love talking about loving jazz."[50] For Silman, the use of "musical taste . . . as a signifier for emotional depth" is a problematic trope in cinema that *La La Land*, with its primarily white male creative team, perpetuates.

The gender dynamics at play more broadly in the representation of the leading couple were also critiqued. Morgan Leigh Davies compared *La La Land*'s protagonists to those in Chazelle's earlier films, suggesting that they "paint the artistic life as masculine . . . men have power, and they get (almost) everything they want. . . . And women? All they get to do is listen."[51] Specifically, for Davies, Chazelle's "masochistic, obsessive, self-righteous, and aggressively male" depiction of the artistic process results in Mia's being a less fleshed out character than Sebastian. Sebastian is "the author of their relationship," and Chazelle privileges his voice over hers. Richard Brody of the *New Yorker* claimed that Chazelle turns Mia "into an absolute cipher, giving her nothing whatsoever to talk about. . . . Chazelle is interested in Mia not as a character or as a person but as an ornament, a symbol of a kind of dream and a kind of success, and he puts her into his film empty, leaving her to be filled solely by the personality and the talent of Stone herself."[52] In other words, although the acting abilities of Gosling and Stone might have added dimension to the characters, Seb and Mia were written in ways that reinscribed problematic representations of women and gender dynamics that have pervaded Hollywood since the era of the classic film musical. Furthermore, for critic Abby Olcese, the couple's conflict was just not compelling enough: "to put it simply, their problems . . . aren't problems. . . . These are, at best, first-world problems. Not only do they make the story less interesting, they make the characters seem petty as well."[53]

It is likely that *La La Land* would not have received nearly as much backlash had it not become such a darling of critics and fans and a frontrunner for the Best Picture Academy Award. The fact that it could seemingly do no wrong at first made it an easy target. But as a film, it also seemed to perfectly encapsulate many of the problems that Hollywood had been contending with in the preceding years, as I detail below. The whiteness of the Academy, and the predominance of white, male writers and directors in Hollywood, had caused even well-intentioned people to reinscribe stereotypes and tired tropes around race and gender in celebrated films; *La La Land* seemed to epitomize this very phenomenon.

La La Land and the Oscars

La La Land's reception was further shaped by the 89th Academy Awards, and the chaotic events that unfolded that evening left an indelible mark on the film's place in popular culture. Throughout the festival and awards show circuit in 2016 and early 2017, *La La Land* had consistently been shown alongside Barry Jenkins's *Moonlight*. With a much more modest $1.5 million budget, *Moonlight* depicted the coming of age of a young Black man, exploring the difficulties he faces because of his sexuality and his drug-abusing mother. It was the first LGBTQ film with an all-Black cast, and it was lauded by critics as one of the best films of the year (and has since gained status as one of the best films of the 21st century to date).[54] In many ways, *La La Land* and *Moonlight* could not be more different—the former is big-budget, splashy, with famous stars and an almost entirely white cast and creative team, while the latter is small, intimate, and intense, with a lesser-known Black cast and writer/director. Both were nominated for multiple Oscars, including Best Picture.

The 2017 Oscars not only took place in the shadow of President Trump's election, which led to a greater politicization of the awards show,[55] but it was also the first Academy Awards after the trending of the hashtag #OscarsSoWhite. In both 2015 and 2016, all twenty Academy Award acting nominations went to white actors. #OscarsSoWhite, which gained widespread traction leading up to the 2016 Oscars, was intended to point out the homogeneity of the governing body granting awards, which had an impact on the kinds of stories that were valued and the ways these stories were told. On the heels of #BlackLivesMatter, #OscarsSoWhite prompted a broader discussion among the film industry about the desperate need for more diversity and inclusion in Hollywood.[56] The Academy's board of governors responded by taking "dramatic steps" to change the demographic of their membership,[57] but by the 2017 Oscars, it was not yet clear whether this had made any difference.

In this context, *La La Land* and *Moonlight* as nominees for Best Picture took on more symbolic significance, one as the kind of movie that seemed tailor-made for the Academy of years past—a Hollywood movie that is a love letter to Hollywood (from a white male perspective)—and the other as the kind of movie that had for so long been overlooked by the Academy. Both films won Oscars that night: *La La Land* won Best Director (Chazelle), Best Actress (Stone), Best Original Score (Hurwitz), Best Song (Hurwitz, Pasek, and Paul), Best Cinematography (Linus Sandgren), and Best Production Design, while *Moonlight* won Best Adapted Screenplay (Jenkins) and Best Supporting Actor (Mahershala Ali). When it came to the Best Picture award, *La La Land*'s success at the Golden Globes and other awards shows made its

Oscar win seem to be a foregone conclusion, but one that, for many, signaled the continued conservatism and irrelevance of the Academy despite its efforts to diversify. David Sims had predicted in December 2016 that *La La Land* would do well at the Oscars, making "another year of escapism" the favorite for February, despite the institutional changes under way.[58]

Indeed, no one blinked an eye when the inevitable happened: Warren Beatty and Faye Dunaway opened the envelope to announce Best Picture, and after Beatty paused dramatically, Dunaway announced that *La La Land* had won. But no one was prepared for the chaos of the few minutes that followed. Members of the cast and creative team walked up to the stage, and the producers began making their acceptance speeches. A few minutes later, it became apparent that something was wrong, as crew members came onstage and took the envelopes. Producer Fred Berger wrapped up his speech by saying, "We lost, by the way." Then producer Jordan Horowitz stepped to the microphone and announced the error: "I'm sorry, no, there's a mistake. *Moonlight*, you guys won Best Picture." Off microphone, he said to the *Moonlight* crew, "This is not a joke," and ushered them onstage, while they attempted, bewildered, to shift gears (Figure 5.2). Host Jimmy Kimmel tried to crack a joke, while Beatty explained that he and Dunaway had mistakenly been given the card for Best Actress. Never before had the incorrect film been announced for Best Picture, making the event a historic blunder.[59]

Figure 5.2 *La La Land* producer Jordan Horowitz holds up the Best Picture envelope at the 2017 Academy Awards

It was an embarrassing mistake for the producers of the Academy Awards show that night. Brooks Barnes and Cara Buckley of the *New York Times* wrote that the debacle "warped and dampened the euphoria of film executives and artists who had spent years working on the two movies."[60] But more than that, the *La La Land*/*Moonlight* mix-up symbolized something greater about the state of representation in Hollywood. It overshadowed *Moonlight*'s historic win[61] and left what Leila Jordan called a "disappointing legacy" for *La La Land*:

> *La La Land* and *Moonlight* will never be able to be appreciated for the movies they are without being tied to that one moment and each other. And as the Oscars struggle to retain viewership, the moment has become its last hurrah of relevance, albeit in an embarrassing manner....
>
> [S]ome of the lasting criticism of *La La Land* seems to be rooted in the 2017 flub. While some hated it from the start, after that moment no one wanted to lend the film any kindness. *La La Land* became the villain, the usurper that tried to steal the award away. *La La Land* is symbolic of a film that just assumes it will receive praise through its subject matter....
>
> *Moonlight* got its big moment stolen for a reason completely out of its control. The emotional impact was diminished by everyone still being in shock that such a mistake even happened....
>
> *Moonlight* deserved better than the win it got.[62]

Through no fault of its own, *La La Land* ended up robbing *Moonlight* of its historic moment. But the fact that critics had already identified problems in its representation seemed to implicate it in the Oscars mix-up, making it forever symbolize the old guard of Hollywood, of problematic, navel-gazing, white male nostalgia.

La La Land's Cultural Impact

La La Land's reception over the course of 2016 and early 2017—from film festival darling, to award-winner, to problematic film, to stealer of *Moonlight*'s thunder—represents the tumultuous cultural time in which it premiered. It was a time when Hollywood, and U.S. culture more broadly, was reckoning with a shifting political landscape and grappling with its own implication in the stereotyping and exclusion of marginalized identities. For many, *La La*

Land epitomized a kind of thoughtless exclusion—through the whiteness of the leading couple, Seb's relationship to jazz, and the film's nostalgia for an earlier era—that Hollywood had been guilty of for years.

Yet it is worth remembering that throughout its tumultuous reception, *La La Land* also continued to amass countless fans, who forgave its flaws because of the ways it resonated with them. Whether it was the celebration of the classic Hollywood musical after years of the form lying (more or less) dormant, the raw realness of the leading couple's choice between love and career, or the catchy music and visually stunning mise-en-scène and cinematography, it resonated, and continues to resonate, for many. It is also doubtful that the film would have amassed such a strong backlash had it not first become such a beloved cultural phenomenon. *La La Land's* status as a bellwether for the future of the Hollywood musical is far from clear. But by bringing many ongoing debates about the film musical into the contemporary age, it has shown how the genre is uniquely situated to function as a lightning rod for broader cultural conversations.

Conclusion

La La Land's Legacy

In Season 4, Episode 13 of *Crazy Ex-Girlfriend* ("I Have to Get Out," 2019), protagonist Rebecca talks with her therapist about her reluctance to take anti-depressants. Her therapist reassures her that "lots of people" are on them. Upbeat musical accompaniment with a familiar-sounding syncopated rhythm begins to underscore her monologue, until Rebecca's therapist leads them out into the reception area. There, three brightly dressed patients sit reading magazines, lowering them one by one to sing the names of medications to Rebecca: "Fluoxetine, fluoxetine, Paroxetine, paroxetine, Citalopram, citalopram, Take once a day." Thus begins the song "Anti-Depressants Are So Not a Big Deal," a musical parody of *La La Land*'s "Another Day of Sun." The references to *La La Land*'s opening number are numerous—in addition to the similarities in melodic, rhythmic, and harmonic material and the use of full symphonic accompaniment combined with jazz orchestration, the scene features dancers in colorful costumes and uses a 360-degree arc shot to capture the choreography of the neighbors who have gathered to help sing the song. Each episode of *Crazy Ex-Girlfriend* was a musical, featuring at least two original songs. But the parody of *La La Land* for this specific song was intentional: "Another Day of Sun" depicts Los Angeles as full of people pursuing their dreams against all odds, while "Anti-Depressants Are So Not a Big Deal" reinforces that the only commonality the residents of West Covina, California, share is their use of anti-depressants. The song won *Crazy Ex-Girlfriend* an Emmy Award for Outstanding Music and Lyrics.

The fact that the scene was such a recognizable parody of "Another Day of Sun" reveals just how pervasive a cultural phenomenon *La La Land* had become in the years immediately following its release. Its musical and choreographic style, and even its camerawork, were distinctive enough to be instantly recognizable in the parody. The send-up also functions to some extent as an homage, lovingly pointing to the tension between *La La Land*'s

La La Land. Hannah Lewis, Oxford University Press. © Oxford University Press 2024.
DOI: 10.1093/9780197682616.003.0007

sunny upbeat number and its cynicism: "Anti-Depressants Are So Not a Big Deal" similarly plays on the incongruity between its upbeat music and choreography and the pragmatism of its lyrics.

La La Land was certainly a cinematic sensation and a cultural phenomenon when it first premiered. It was augured to usher in a new era for the film musical genre, in a similar way to *Moulin Rouge!* (2001) fifteen years earlier. Instead of inspiring a spate of original musical films, however, *Moulin Rouge!* was followed by almost two decades of stage-to-screen adaptations. In historical hindsight, the significance of *Moulin Rouge!* was as much about how the film musical genre intersected with Baz Luhrmann's distinctive directorial style as it was about what it did for the genre more broadly. Will the same be true of *La La Land*? Will it be remembered more for what it revealed about Chazelle's style than for its influence on the film musical? It is too early to tell.

La La Land was also not the only screen media of the past decade to draw on the audiovisual aesthetics of the classic film musical, though it was rather singular in its approach. Most recent homages to the classic Hollywood musical fall more under the category of parody, such as the Coen Brothers' film *Hail, Caesar!* (2016) and the Apple TV series *Schmigadoon!* (2021). In contrast, *La La Land*'s approach to homage is much more serious, and more expressive, because its use of generic conventions is as a sincere conduit of feelings. No film or television show has yet emulated *La La Land*'s particular approach, except in parody, but it is too soon to determine the scope of its influence. Although several high-profile film musicals have premiered in the years following *La La Land*, including the original *The Greatest Showman* (2017) and the adaptations of *In the Heights* (2021) and *West Side Story* (2021), these productions were already in the works by the time of *La La Land*'s massive success, so the extent of its influence on future Hollywood musicals remains to be seen.

Even now, however, *La La Land*'s impact continues to be felt. The attention it still receives on social media platforms like TikTok speaks to its large and growing fan base. The film's music has had its own afterlife, as the award-winning, chart-topping soundtrack continues to be tremendously successful. "La La Land in Concert," a screening of the film featuring a live orchestra performing the score, has toured the world, and medleys of its songs have been arranged for concert band and chorus. And, at the time of this writing, it has just been announced that the film will be adapted into a Broadway musical, which will bring its story and music to new audiences.[1]

Whether or not *La La Land* ultimately influences future approaches to the film musical genre, it has already left an indelible mark on film history. Both in its tremendous strengths and in the elements that have received the most pushback, it captured the cultural zeitgeist of a genre and an industry in transition—one that, like Mia and Seb, and like Hurwitz and Chazelle, must decide whether to look backward or keep moving forward.

Notes

Series Editor's Foreword

1. Scott, "Review: Ryan Gosling and Emma Stone Aswirl in Tra La La Land."

Introduction

1. Dargis, "'La La Land' Makes Musicals Matter Again."

Chapter 1

1. The reflexive narrative trope of putting on a show—the subgenre of the "backstage musical"—is pervasive in Hollywood musicals. These films come from the same aesthetic world that *La La Land* nods to, making the parallels between art and life even more fitting.
2. Chazelle has written screenplays for other films: *The Last Exorcism Part II* (2013), *Grand Piano* (2013), and *10 Cloverfield Lane* (2016). But as director, he has always worked with Hurwitz.
3. Dowd, "*Whiplash* Maestro Damien Chazelle on Drumming, Directing, and J. K. Simmons."
4. Damien Chazelle, interview with the author (via Zoom), July 20, 2020.
5. Ibid.
6. Ibid.
7. Legrand described the sung-through aesthetic of the film, where the tempo mimicked that of speech, as "transposed realism" ("*réalisme transposé*"), an interesting parallel with Chazelle's concept of a "realist musical." See *Les Parapluies de Cherbourg* Press File, 23.
8. For more on Demy's musical style, see Stilwell, "Le Demy-monde"; Lindeperg and Marshall, "Time, History and Memory in *Les Parapluies de Cherbourg*"; Duggan, *Queer Enchantments*, 13–41; Powrie and Cadalanu, *The French Film Musical*, 159–174; and Williams, *Republic of Images*, 354–378.
9. Chazelle, interview with the author (via Zoom), July 20, 2020.
10. Ibid.
11. Justin Hurwitz, interview with the author (via Zoom), July 29, 2020.
12. Ibid.
13. Ibid.
14. Ibid.
15. Ibid.
16. Ibid.
17. Howland, *Hearing Luxe Pop.*
18. "Tribeca '09 Interview."
19. Lincoln, "What You Should Know About Damien Chazelle's Little-Seen First Film, *Guy and Madeline on a Park Bench.*"
20. "Tribeca '09 Interview"; Kim, "Student Work Featured at NYC Tribeca Film Festival"; Office for the Arts at Harvard, Artist Development Fellowship, Past Fellows (accessed December 29, 2021), https://ofa.fas.harvard.edu/artist-development-fellowship. According to a *Harvard Crimson* article from the time, "Chazelle could not have realized his project without continuing support from the Harvard community. A fellow VES [Visual and Environmental Studies] concentrator, Jasmine A. McGlade '07 produced 'Guy and Madeline,' while his former roommate Justin G. Hurwitz '08 composed the score. Even now in Los Angeles, Chazelle is living with

other students from Harvard. 'There's still a kind of community that continues after gradua-tion.'" Lind and Schuetz, "The Scenic Route."

21. The film was released on DVD in 2011.
22. Chazelle, interview with the author (via Zoom), July 20, 2020.
23. Ibid.
24. Justin Hurwitz, interview with the author (via Zoom), July 29, 2020.
25. The transition from rhyming dialogue into song has been a common tactic in film musicals, per-haps beginning with the early film musical *Love Me Tonight* (1932).
26. See Chapter 3 for a discussion of *La La Land*'s use of CinemaScope.
27. Morris, "Movie Review: Guy and Madeline on a Park Bench."
28. Hammond, "Damien Chazelle's 'La La Land,' An Ode to Musicals, Romance & L.A., Ready to Launch Venice and Oscar Season." See also Radish, " 'La La Land' Writer/Director Damien Chazelle on Reviving 'Old Hollywood' Techniques."
29. Chazelle, interview with the author (via Zoom), July 20, 2020.
30. Ibid. It is also worth noting that there is a long tradition of Hollywood films about Hollywood and, even more specifically, of Hollywood musicals about Hollywood, which might have made the project more attractive to producers.
31. Hurwitz, interview with the author (via Zoom), July 29, 2020. Hurwitz says that they were "ab-solutely 100 percent sure" about "Mia & Sebastian's Theme," which was "completely locked in," but that all other songs were either thrown out or repurposed.
32. According to Chazelle (interview with the author via Zoom, July 20, 2020), an executive who worked at Focus Features had seen and enjoyed *Guy and Madeline*. This executive gave Chazelle advice about developing a new idea for a film musical, and later introduced him to Berger and Horowitz.
33. Both Berger and Horowitz grew up in Westchester, New York, both even playing for a Jewish temple league basketball team. Berger graduated from the University of Pennsylvania in 2003 and Horowitz from Northwestern University in 2002. They both moved to New York after graduating to work in the film industry, then relocated to Los Angeles around the same time. See Artsy, "From Vision to Reality: Landing 'La La' on the Big Screen"; Hautman, "Jordan Horowitz: 5 Things to Know About the 'La La Land' Producer Who Graciously Cleared Up #EnvelopeGate"; and Wilson, "The Man Behind the La La Magic."
34. Ford, "How 'La La Land' Went from First-Screening Stumbles to Hollywood Ending." According to Fred Berger, "From day one—this was well before *Whiplash*—we knew [Chazelle] was the real deal and felt very strongly that his vision for the movie, while potentially challenging, should get made. Jordan, Damien and myself made a pact that under no circumstances will [Emma and Ryan's characters] end up together in the end. He will always play jazz and not a more acceptable form of music; she will always be an actress, this will always be a love letter to L.A.—we're not relocating to Paris." Ford, "Oscars: 'La La Land' Producer on Making a Pact to Never Change the Film's Ending."
35. On Buddy Rich and *Whiplash*, see Hyfler, "Whiplash, or the Limits of Abuse."
36. Chazelle, interview with the author (via Zoom), July 20, 2020.
37. Hipes and Patten, "Ryan Gosling & Emma Stone Circling Damien Chazelle's 'La La Land.' "
38. Tingen, "Inside Track: *La La Land*."
39. Ahmed, "Inside the Magic of 'La La Land' with Music Director Marius de Vries."
40. Tingen, "Inside Track: *La La Land*."
41. Benj Pasek and Justin Paul, phone interview with the author, August 27, 2020.
42. Lincoln, "For the *La La Land* Lyricists, Getting Hired Was Like Looking in the Mirror."
43. Pasek and Paul, phone interview with the author, August 27, 2020.
44. Mandy Moore, interview with the author (via Zoom), August 21, 2020.
45. Ibid.
46. Ibid. See also Fung, "For Choreographer Mandy Moore, 'La La Land' Was 'the Super Bowl of My Career.' "
47. Moore, interview with the author (via Zoom), August 21, 2020.
48. Easter, " 'La La Land's' Creative Team Goes Behind the Scenes of the Ryan Gosling, Emma Stone Musical."
49. See, for instance, Ford, "How 'La La Land' Went from First-Screening Stumbles to Hollywood Ending." Teller and Watson were announced in the press in 2014, but by 2015, Stone's and Gosling's names were attached to the project: Schmidlin, "Interview: Director Damien Chazelle

Talks 'Whiplash,' Musical Editing & His 'MGM-Style' Musical 'La La Land' "; Hipes and Patten, "Ryan Gosling & Emma Stone Circling Damien Chazelle's 'La La Land.' "

50. Chazelle, interview with the author (via Zoom), July 20, 2020.
51. Artsy, "From Vision to Reality: Landing 'La La' on the Big Screen."
52. Wilson, "The Man Behind the La La Magic"; Howard, "'La La Land' Producer Marc Platt on Damien Chazelle's Love of Filmmaking."
53. Moore, interview with the author (via Zoom), August 21, 2020.
54. According to multiple accounts, everyone involved seemed genuinely impressed at Gosling's ability to learn piano at such a high level of artistry so quickly. See, for instance, ABC News, "John Legend Reveals What Made Him Jealous of Ryan Gosling"; Cine Extras, "La La Land 2016—Behind the Scenes—Ryan Gosling: Piano Student."
55. Chazelle, interview with the author (via Zoom), July 20, 2020.
56. Ford, "Oscars: 'La La Land' Producer on Making a Pact to Never Change the Film's Ending."
57. Chazelle, interview with the author (via Zoom), July 20, 2020.
58. Hurwitz, interview with the author (via Zoom), July 29, 2020.
59. De Vries and Loughrey, "La La Land: Here's a Track-by-Track Breakdown of the Soundtrack by the Film's Music Director."
60. Moore, interview with the author (via Zoom), August 21, 2020.
61. Hurwitz, interview with the author (via Zoom), July 29, 2020. Hurwitz describes "Planetarium" as the one exception; that number got shortened quite a bit during post-production, which frustrated him because it resulted in musical phrases he would not have written, which he characterized as abrupt, underdeveloped, or otherwise musically inelegant.
62. Howard, "'La La Land' Producer Marc Platt on Damien Chazelle's Love of Filmmaking."
63. Hurwitz, interview with the author (via Zoom), July 29, 2020.
64. Ibid.
65. Ibid.
66. Rees, "Interview: Marius de Vries, Musical Director of *La La Land*."
67. Hurwitz, interview with the author (via Zoom), July 29, 2020.
68. Chazelle, phone interview with the author, September 4, 2020.
69. Hurwitz, interview with the author (via Zoom), July 29, 2020.
70. Chazelle, phone interview with the author, September 4, 2020.

Chapter 2

1. Garcia, *The Movie Musical*, 9.
2. Boym, *The Future of Nostalgia*, xiii. Portions of this paragraph are drawn from Lewis, "The Virtuosic Camera."
3. Carew, "Same Old Song," 10.
4. Portions of this paragraph are drawn from Lewis, "The Virtuosic Camera."
5. On the role of nostalgia in the film musical genre, see Altman, *The American Film Musical*, 332–333.
6. Rush, "Recycled Culture," 5. Rush provides a very helpful literature review of the history of the concept of intertextuality, 22–46.
7. Rush, "Oh, What a Beautiful Mormon."
8. Ibid., 48.
9. See, for instance, Dunne, *Intertextual Encounters in American Fiction, Film, and Popular Culture.*
10. *Remembrance Cinema Program* (2003), Australian Center for the Moving Image, quoted in Verevis, *Film Remakes*, 139.
11. Dunne, *Intertextual Encounters*, 1.
12. Verevis, *Film Remakes*, 174.
13. On this phenomenon, see, for instance, Nerdwriter1, "Intertextuality: Hollywood's New Currency."
14. See, for instance, Harris, "*La La Land*'s Many References to Classic Movies: A Guide"; Preciado, "La La Land—Movie References."
15. Damien Chazelle, interview with the author (via Zoom), July 20, 2020.

16. The term "classic Hollywood" is still commonly used in scholarly contexts as well as in popular parlance. David Bordwell, Janet Staiger, and Kristin Thompson's 1985 book *The Classical Hollywood Cinema: Film Style and Mode of Production to 1960* continues to be influential and has cemented the term's scholarly relevance, despite its potential problems or pitfalls.

17. Damien Chazelle, interview with the author (via Zoom), July 20, 2020.

18. Ibid.

19. Altman, *The American Film Musical*, 19.

20. Ibid., 20. "Each partner is seen as potentially complete but unable to actualize one side of his/her personality; marriage serves to provide each lover with the perfect complement, the one person capable of giving life to the repressed component in a dualistic psychic configuration" (82).

21. Ibid., 49.

22. Dabrowska, "La La Land (Damien Chazelle, US)—Special Presentations."

23. Cohan, *Hollywood Musicals*, 205. Alissa Wilkinson suggests that the film is a "shot of optimism that's been dosed with realism," in "La La Land Sees Old Hollywood Magic Giving Way to Modern Melancholy."

24. Altman, *The American Film Musical*, 207.

25. Ibid., 200.

26. Feuer, "The Self-Reflective Musical and the Myth of Entertainment," 160.

27. Feuer, *The Hollywood Musical*, 8.

28. Ibid., 4.

29. According to popular accounts, the cast of *La La Land* watched *Singin' in the Rain* every day on set for inspiration. Whether or not this is actually true, it is clear that *La La Land* owes much of its structure, narrative, and style to *Singin' in the Rain*. *Singin' in the Rain* is itself satirical and referential, representing the 1920s from a decidedly 1950s perspective—another point of influence for *La La Land*, which uses Golden Age aesthetics to represent the 2010s. See Roschke, "Singin' in the Rain Impacted La La Land More Than You Think."

30. Chazelle, interview with the author (via Zoom), July 27, 2020.

31. Ibid.

32. In *The Smiling Lieutenant*, Maurice Chevalier, playing a Viennese lieutenant, is in love with Franzi (Claudette Colbert's character), but he must marry the Princess of Flausenthurm (Miriam Hopkins) to avoid an international incident. The Princess is very much in love with the Lieutenant, and when Franzi sees this, she helps transform the Princess by giving her a makeover, sacrificing her own happiness in order to make the couple happy.

33. Justin Hurwitz, interview with the author (via Zoom), July 29, 2020.

34. Scott, "Review: Ryan Gosling and Emma Stone Aswirl in Tra La La Land."

35. Chazelle, interview with the author (via Zoom), July 20, 2020.

36. Fung, "For Choreographer Mandy Moore, 'La La Land' Was 'the Super Bowl of My Career.'"

37. Chazelle, interview with the author (via Zoom), July 20, 2020.

38. Justin Paul, phone interview with the author, August 27, 2020.

39. Benj Pasek, phone interview with the author, August 27, 2020.

40. Chazelle, interview with the author (via Zoom), July 27, 2020.

41. Ibid.

42. Hurwitz, interview with the author (via Zoom), July 29, 2020. Many musical theater composers have utilized mode mixture to various effects. One example is the song "At the Ballet" in *A Chorus Line*, in which the dancers describe their family traumas and how ballet was always a safe and happy refuge for them.

43. Mandy Moore, interview with the author (via Zoom), August 21, 2020.

44. Chazelle, interview with the author (via Zoom), July 27, 2020.

45. Moore, interview with the author (via Zoom), August 21, 2020.

46. Ibid.

47. In musicals, a couple that sings or dances together is seen to be a good romantic match, while if they do not do so, they do not seem to naturally belong together. Andrea Most argues that if a leading couple does not sing a duet together, they are seen as fundamentally incompatible. Most, *Making Americans*, 171.

48. According to Justin Hurwitz, the song was originally written for Mia to sing: "We flipped it. It was going to be Mia taking a stroll, thinking about new love and being apprehensive, and reflecting on some of the dreams and the loves from the past that didn't work. But it's the same idea." Hurwitz, interview with the author (via Zoom), July 29, 2020.

49. Ibid.

50. Chazelle, phone interview with the author, September 4, 2020.
51. In film, a dream ballet choreographed by Katherine Dunham was featured in *Stormy Weather* in the same year. On *La La Land*'s dream ballet, see Gardner, "Revealing the Subconscious."
52. Robinette, "'La La Land': Go Inside the Epilogue."
53. Chazelle, phone interview with the author, September 4, 2020.
54. Chazelle, interview with the author (via Zoom), July 27, 2020.
55. Chazelle, phone interview with the author, September 4, 2020.
56. Keller, "La La Land."
57. Garrett, "'La La Land' Refurbished the Classic Musical Format for a Modern Audience."
58. Voeltz, "'The Joke's on History.'"
59. Nelson, "The Unbearable Whiteness of *La La Land*."

Chapter 3

 1. McMillin, *The Musical as Drama*, 6.
 2. From Rudolph Arnheim to André Bazin to Siegfried Kracauer and beyond, there has long been a strain of film theory that has prized cinematic realism, believing cinema's essence to be its ability for realistic representation. (This view of cinema is in contrast with other filmmakers and theorists who emphasize cinema's potential for manipulating reality.)
 3. Portions of this chapter are drawn from Lewis, "The Virtuosic Camera."
 4. Wilkinson, "La La Land Sees Old Hollywood Magic Giving Way to Modern Melancholy."
 5. Damien Chazelle, interview with the author (via Zoom), July 20, 2020.
 6. Ibid.
 7. Ibid.
 8. Ibid.
 9. McMillin, *The Musical as Drama*, 2. See also Lewis, "*Love Me Tonight* (1932) and the Development of the Integrated Film Musical."
10. Feuer, *The Hollywood Musical*, 13.
11. Fred Astaire, quoted in Mueller, *Astaire Dancing*, 26.
12. Brideson and Brideson, *He's Got Rhythm*, 271–272; Hess and Dabholkar, *Singin' in the Rain*, 135.
13. Feuer, *The Hollywood Musical*, 35–36, 42–44.
14. See Clover, "Dancin' in the Rain."
15. Muir, *Singing a New Tune*, 3.
16. Knapp, "Getting Real," 56.
17. Kessler, *Destabilizing the Hollywood Musical*.
18. Muir, *Singing a New Tune*, 77.
19. On the resurgence of the film musical, see Muir, *Singing a New Tune*; and Rodosthenous, *Twenty-First Century Musicals*.
20. Vernallis, "Accelerated Aesthetics," 707. See also Richardson, Gorbman, and Vernallis, *The Oxford Handbook of New Audiovisual Aesthetics*.
21. Bordwell, "Intensified Continuity," 20.
22. Ibid. The 2019 British war epic *1917* is an extreme example, as it was filmed in long takes and elaborately moving shots to appear as if it unfolds in one continuous take.
23. King, "Spectacle, Narrative, and the Spectacular Hollywood Blockbuster," 117.
24. On the music video aesthetic, see Vernallis, *Experiencing Music Video*; Vernallis, *Unruly Media*.
25. On the audiovisual style of *Moulin Rouge!*, see Ingram, "It's a Little Bit Funny"; Vernallis, *Unruly Media*, 76–93; Yang, "*Moulin Rouge!* and the Undoing of Opera"; and Stilwell, "Theatricality, Artifice, and Affective Space in the Works of Baz Luhrmann."
26. "Shot in CinemaScope, La La Land Vibrantly Romances the Olden Days of Hollywood."
27. Chazelle, interview with the author (via Zoom), July 27, 2020. At the same time, he claims that while working on *La La Land*, he began to appreciate thoughtful cutting and how "cutting could help."
28. Ibid.
29. Bordwell, "Intensified Continuity," 20.
30. "How *La La Land* Pulled Off That Stunning Highway Dance Sequence"; "'La La Land' High-Flying Highway Opening Scene."
31. Robertson, "Feminist Camp in *Gold Diggers of 1933*," 131.

32. See Barrios, *A Song in the Dark*, 371–407; Dinerstein, *Swinging the Machine*, 202–220; Robertson, "Feminist Camp in *Gold Diggers of 1933*"; Roth, "Some Warners Musicals and the Spirit of the New Deal."
33. See Chapter 2, note 47.
34. Calvario, "'La La Land' Composer Justin Hurwitz Breaks Down Emma Stone's Passionate 'Audition' Song." In this number, there are many resonances with Anne Hathaway's performance of "I Dreamed a Dream" in the role of Fantine in *Les Misérables*: the number is filmed in a long take, in close-up, with on-set singing.
35. Cunningham, "The Making of 'La La Land.'"
36. See Watkins, "Oscar Frontrunner 'La La Land' Is a Good Movie, but a Bad Musical."
37. Piccini, "The Greatest Showmen."
38. Chow, "How 3 Key *In the Heights* Scenes Were Reimagined from Stage to Screen."
39. O'Falt, "'In the Heights': How They Danced Up the Side of a Building"; Go Creative Show, "'When the Sun Goes Down' Breakdown—IN THE HEIGHTS (Show Short)."
40. See, for instance, Gibbs, "Synthesizers, Virtual Orchestras, and Ableton Live."

Chapter 4

1. Damien Chazelle, interview with the author (via Zoom), July 27, 2020.
2. See Ake, Garrett, and Goldmark, *Jazz/Not Jazz*.
3. As Gabriel Solis suggests, "Baby Boomers and Generation Xers invested heavily in a discourse of genre purity as a way of attaching value to their chosen object of attention"; Solis, "Soul, Afrofuturism & the Timeliness of Contemporary Jazz Fusions," 24. See also DeVeaux, "Constructing the Jazz Tradition."
4. Chinen, *Playing Changes*, 5.
5. Fellezs, *Birds of Fire*.
6. Chambers, "*La La Land* Is Clueless About What's Actually Happening in Jazz."
7. Chinen, "The Gig: Behold the Jazzbro."
8. Graham, "Jazzbros: A Force for Jazzgood or Jazzevil?"
9. Ratliff, "Jazz Hate."
10. Chazelle, interview with the author (via Zoom), July 27, 2020.
11. Ibid.
12. Hurwitz, interview with the author (via Zoom), July 30, 2020.
13. Chazelle, interview with the author (via Zoom), July 27, 2020.
14. Ibid. According to some accounts, Chazelle at one point offered the role to actor Michael B. Jordan; Riley, "'La La Land.'" I have found no other specific mentions of other Black actors who were considered for the role.
15. Jon Caramanica expresses a similar sentiment when he writes, "On the surface, [Chazelle] treats jazz as an object of affection, but really it's not much more than a stand-in for white male self-flagellation, a proxy for how white men come to understand themselves"; "Does 'La La Land' Get Jazz, or Exploit It?"
16. Gabbard, "*La La Land* Is a Hit, but Is It Good for Jazz?," 101.
17. Decker, "Race, Ethnicity, Performance," 199.
18. Knight, *Disintegrating the Musical*, 1.
19. See Woll, *Black Musical Theatre*.
20. On blackface minstrelsy and American popular music, see, for instance, Lott, *Love and Theft*; Cockrell, *Demons of Disorder*; Johnson, *Burnt Cork*; and Morrison, "Race, Blacksound, and the (Re)making of Musicological Discourse."
21. Rogin, *Blackface, White Noise*.
22. Gabbard, *Jammin' at the Margins*, 10.
23. Decker, *Music Makes Me*.
24. Ibid., 274.
25. Ibid., 275.
26. Clover, "Dancin' in the Rain," 742.
27. Ibid., 740.
28. Madison, "'La La Land''s White Jazz Narrative."
29. Graham, "Jazzbros."

30. Williams, "John Legend—Legend in La La Land!"
31. Ibid.
32. Barnard, "John Legend on Acting for La La Land."
33. Chazelle, phone interview with the author, September 4, 2020.
34. Marchese, "*La La Land* Director Damien Chazelle Breaks Down Jazz's Popularity Problem."
35. Ibid.
36. Williams, "John Legend—Legend in La La Land!"
37. Chazelle, phone interview with the author, September 4, 2020.
38. Ibid.
39. Roschke, "John Legend Laughed at Me When I Asked If Ryan Gosling Came to Him for Piano Tips."
40. Chazelle, phone interview with the author, September 4, 2020.
41. Newman, "John Legend on Producing & Acting in 'La La Land,' Broadway Plans, 'Role Model' Quincy Jones." Elsewhere he claimed it needed to be a "viable option" (Barnard, "John Legend on Acting for La La Land").
42. Hurwitz, interview with the author (via Zoom), July 30, 2020.
43. Chambers, "*La La Land* Is Clueless About What's Actually Happening in Jazz."
44. Moore, interview with the author (via Zoom), August 21, 2020.
45. Maner, *To Pimp a Butterfly*, 5–6; Hobbs, "The History of the West Coast Get Down, LA's Jazz Giants"; Tate, "Why Jazz Will Always Be Relevant."
46. Hobbs, "The History of the West Coast Get Down."
47. Ibid.
48. Walls, "Is Jazz Entering a New Golden Age?"
49. Tate, "Why Jazz Will Always Be Relevant."

Chapter 5

 1. Saturday Night Live, "La La Land Interrogation—SNL."
 2. "Love 'La La Land'? Hate It? So Do We."
 3. Vivarelli, "'La La Land' Opens 73rd Venice Film Festival on Upbeat Note Despite Tight Security."
 4. Desta, "*La La Land* Stuns at the Venice Film Festival."
 5. Ibid.
 6. Barna, "'La La Land' Opens the Venice Film Festival, Leaving Critics Breathless."
 7. Hopewell, "Ryan Gosling, Emma Stone, Damien Chazelle's 'La La Land' Wow Venice."
 8. McCarthy, "'La La Land': Venice Review."
 9. Gleiberman, "Film Review: 'La La Land.'"
10. McCarthy, "La La Land."
11. Hammond, "'La La Land' Review."
12. Gleiberman, "Film Review: 'La La Land.'"
13. Zacharek, "Do You Hate Musicals? The Dazzling *La La Land* Could Change That."
14. Bradshaw, "La La Land Review."
15. Hammond, "'La La Land' Review."
16. Tiziana Mantovani, quoted in Hopewell, "Ryan Gosling, Emma Stone, Damien Chazelle's 'La La Land' Wow Venice."
17. Zacharek, "Do You Hate Musicals?"
18. Barna, "'La La Land' Opens the Venice Film Festival."
19. Feinberg, "Telluride: 'La La Land' Opens to Big Applause."
20. Nolfi, "Telluride Film Festival."
21. Lawson, "*La La Land* Is a Wonder, and Another Big Breakthrough for Emma Stone."
22. Scott, "Cinema Is Dead? Telluride Says Not Yet."
23. Barnes, "'La La Land' Wins Top Prize at Toronto International Film Festival."
24. Zeitchik, "Toronto 2016."
25. Yuan, "Toronto: Emma Stone and Ryan Gosling's *La La Land* Is the Big Beating Heart of a Movie Musical We've Been Craving."
26. "'La La Land' to Centerpiece Middleburg Film Festival"; Hipes, "'La La Land' Added As AFI Fest Centerpiece Gala."

27. Feinberg, "Telluride: 'La La Land' Opens to Big Applause."
28. Scott, "Cinema Is Dead?"
29. Dargis, "'La La Land' Makes Musicals Matter Again."
30. Lane, "Fun in 'La La Land.'"
31. Truitt, "Review: Prepare to Be Enchanted by Magical Musical 'La La Land.'"
32. LaSalle, "Beautiful, Hopeful 'La La Land' Is One of the Year's Best."
33. Macdonald, "'La La Land' Review: Get Lost in This Dreamy Musical."
34. Truitt, "Review: Prepare to Be Enchanted by Magical Musical 'La La Land.'"
35. Orr, "The Novelty and Nostalgia of *La La Land*."
36. LaSalle, "Beautiful, Hopeful 'La La Land' Is One of the Year's Best."
37. Fleming, Jr., "No 18 'La La Land' Box Office Profits—2016 Most Valuable Movie Blockbuster Tournament."
38. Yahr, "Your Guide to the 'La La Land' Backlash."
39. Lawler, "Oscar Nominations 2017: The Case against 'La La Land.'"
40. Davies, "Art in the Age of Masculinist Hollywood."
41. Robin Pogrebin, quoted in "Love 'La La Land'? Hate It? So Do We."
42. Reed, "Good-Intentioned but Overrated, 'La La Land' Reeks of Mothballs."
43. Ibid.
44. Dargis, "'La La Land' Makes Musicals Matter Again."
45. Nelson, "The Unbearable Whiteness of *La La Land*."
46. Burr, "'La La Land' Resurrects the Classic Movie Musical."
47. Abdul-Jabbar, "How 'La La Land' Misleads on Race, Romance and Jazz."
48. Lott-Lavigna, "La La Land Review: An Ambitious Musical Soured by Racist Undertones." Though the lack of queer characters was less frequently commented upon, it did enter the public discourse on Twitter: Rostam, a musician and producer who was in the band Vampire Weekend, tweeted his frustration that the musical "didn't have a single gay person in it"; quoted in Calvario, "'La La Land': Rostam Criticizes the Musical's Race Narrative and Lack of Queer Characters."
49. Willmore, "The Privilege of Hollywood Nostalgia."
50. Silman, "*La La Land*: A Musical Ode to Men Who Love Loving Jazz."
51. Davies, "Art in the Age of Masculinist Hollywood."
52. Brody, "The Empty Exertions of 'La La Land.'" See also Framke, "Emma Stone's La La Land Performance Transcends the Film's Biggest Flaw"; Nicholson, "'La La Land': A City of Tap-Dancing Angels."
53. Olcese, "'La La Land' Is Dreamy, but a Film in the Wrong Year."
54. Dargis and Scott, "The 25 Best Films of the 21st Century So Far."
55. Buchanan and Horn, "The Oscars Will Be More Political Than Ever, and That's a Good Thing."
56. Izundu, "Oscars So White: What People Are Saying About Diversity in Hollywood"; Ugwu, "The Hashtag That Changed the Oscars: An Oral History."
57. Izundu, "Oscars So White."
58. Sims, "The Lead Contenders for This Year's Oscars."
59. Barnes and Buckley, "'Moonlight,' 'La La Land' and Everything Else That Happened at the Oscars." The events described can be seen at Eyewitness News, "'Moonlight' or 'La La Land'? Best Picture Mix-up at Oscars."
60. Barnes and Buckley, "What It Was Like Onstage During the Oscars 2017 Best Picture Mistake."
61. France, "Oscar Mistake Overshadows Historic Moment for 'Moonlight.'"
62. Jordan, "*Moonlight, La La Land*, and the 2017 Best Picture Oscars Flub, Five Years Later."

Conclusion

1. See Galuppo, "'La La Land' to Become a Broadway Musical." The production will be directed by Bertlett Sher based on a book written by Ayad Akhtar and Matthew Decker, with new songs written by Hurwitz, Pasek, and Paul (Chazelle is not directly involved in the adaptation process). This adaptation falls into a broader trend of Broadway adaptations of Hollywood films, a trend that has intensified in recent years.

Bibliography

Personal Interviews

Chazelle, Damien. Interview with the author (via Zoom), July 20, 2020.
Chazelle, Damien. Interview with the author (via Zoom), July 27, 2020.
Chazelle, Damien. Phone interview with the author, September 4, 2020.
Hurwitz, Justin. Interview with the author (via Zoom), July 29, 2020.
Hurwitz, Justin. Interview with the author (via Zoom), July 30, 2020.
Moore, Mandy. Interview with the author (via Zoom), August 21, 2020.
Pasek, Benj, and Justin Paul. Phone interview with the author, August 27, 2020.

Scholarly Sources

Ake, David, Charles Hiroshi Garrett, and Daniel Goldmark, eds. *Jazz/Not Jazz: The Music and Its Boundaries.* Berkeley: University of California Press, 2012.

Altman, Rick. *The American Film Musical.* Bloomington: Indiana University Press, 1987.

Barrios, Richard. *A Song in the Dark: The Birth of the Musical Film.* New York: Oxford University Press, 1995.

Bordwell, David. "Intensified Continuity: Visual Style in Contemporary American Film." *Film Quarterly* 55, no. 3 (2002): 16–28.

Bordwell, David, Janet Staiger, and Kristin Thompson. *The Classical Hollywood Cinema: Film Style and the Mode of Production to 1960.* London: Routledge, 1985.

Boym, Svetlana. *The Future of Nostalgia.* New York: Basic Books, 2001.

Brideson, Cynthia, and Sara Brideson. *He's Got Rhythm: The Life and Career of Gene Kelly.* Lexington: University Press of Kentucky, 2017.

Carew, Anthony. "Same Old Song: Nostalgia and Fantasy in *La La Land.*" *Screen Education,* no. 90 (September 2018): 10–15.

Chinen, Nate. *Playing Changes: Jazz for the New Century.* New York: Pantheon Books, 2018.

Clover, Carol J. "Dancin' in the Rain." *Critical Inquiry* 21, no. 4 (1995): 722–747.

Cockrell, Dale. *Demons of Disorder: Early Blackface Minstrels and Their World.* Cambridge: Cambridge University Press, 1997.

Cohan, Steven. *Hollywood by Hollywood: The Backstudio Picture and the Mystique of Making Movies.* New York: Oxford University Press, 2019.

Cohan, Steven. *Hollywood Musicals.* New York: Routledge, 2019.

Decker, Todd. *Music Makes Me: Fred Astaire and Jazz.* Berkeley: University of California Press, 2011.

Decker, Todd. "Race, Ethnicity, Performance." In *The Oxford Handbook of the American Musical,* edited by Raymond Knapp, Mitchell Morris, and Stacy Wolf, 197–209. New York: Oxford University Press, 2011.

DeVeaux, Scott. "Constructing the Jazz Tradition: Jazz Historiography." *Black American Literature Forum* 25, no. 3 (Autumn 1991): 525–560.

Dinerstein, Joel. *Swinging the Machine: Modernity, Technology, and African American Culture between the World Wars.* Amherst: University of Massachusetts Press, 2003.

Duggan, Anne E. *Queer Enchantments: Gender, Sexuality, and Class in the Fairy-Tale Cinema of Jacques Demy.* Detroit: Wayne State University Press, 2013.

Dunne, Michael. *Intertextual Encounters in American Fiction, Film, and Popular Culture.* Bowling Green, OH: Bowling Green State University Popular Press, 2001.

Fellezs, Kevin. *Birds of Fire: Jazz, Rock, Funk, and the Creation of Fusion.* Durham, NC: Duke University Press, 2011.

Feuer, Jane. *The Hollywood Musical.* 2nd ed. Bloomington: Indiana University Press, 1993.

Feuer, Jane. "The Self-Reflective Musical and the Myth of Entertainment." In *Genre: The Musical: A Reader,* edited by Rick Altman, 159–174. London: Routledge, 1981.

Gabbard, Krin. *Jammin' at the Margins: Jazz and the American Cinema.* Chicago: University of Chicago Press, 1996.

Gabbard, Krin. "*La La Land* Is a Hit, but Is It Good for Jazz?" *Dædalus* 148, no. 2 (2019): 92–103.

Garcia, Desirée J. *The Movie Musical.* New Brunswick, NJ: Rutgers University Press, 2021.

Gardner, Kara. "Revealing the Subconscious: The Dream Ballet in Movie Musicals." In *The Oxford Handbook of The Hollywood Musical,* edited by Dominic Broomfield-McHugh, 47–71. New York: Oxford University Press, 2022.

Gibbs, Liam E. "Synthesizers, Virtual Orchestras, and Ableton Live: Digitally Rendered Music on Broadway and Musicians' Union Resistance." *Journal of the Society for American Music* 13, no. 3 (August 2019): 273–304.

Hess, Earl J., and Pratibha A. Dabholkar. *Singin' in the Rain: The Making of an American Masterpiece.* Lawrence: University Press of Kansas, 2009.

Howland, John. *Hearing Luxe Pop: Glorification, Glamour, and the Middlebrow in American Popular Music.* Oakland: University of California Press, 2021.

Ingram, Susan. "It's a Little Bit Funny: *Moulin Rouge*'s Sparkling Postmodern Critique." In *Music, Meaning, and Media,* edited by Erkki Pekkilä, David Neumeyer, and Richard Littlefield, 66–74. Imatra: International Semiotics Institute, 2006.

Johnson, Stephen, ed. *Burnt Cork: Traditions and Legacies of Blackface Minstrelsy.* Amherst: University of Massachusetts Press, 2012.

Kessler, Kelly. *Destabilizing the Hollywood Musical: Music, Masculinity and Mayhem.* London: Palgrave Macmillan, 2010.

King, Geoff. "Spectacle, Narrative, and the Spectacular Hollywood Blockbuster." In *Movie Blockbusters,* edited by Julian Stringer, 114–127. London: Routledge, 2003.

Knapp, Raymond. "Getting Real: Stage Musical versus Filmic Realism in Film Adaptations from *Camelot* to *Cabaret.*" In *The Oxford Handbook of Musical Theatre Screen Adaptations,* edited by Dominic McHugh, 55–83. New York: Oxford University Press, 2019.

Knight, Arthur. *Disintegrating the Musical: Black Performance and American Musical Film.* Durham, NC: Duke University Press, 2002.

Lewis, Hannah. "*Love Me Tonight* (1932) and the Development of the Integrated Film Musical." *Musical Quarterly* 100, no. 1 (2017): 3–32.

Lewis, Hannah. "The Virtuosic Camera: Nostalgia, Technology, and the Contemporary Hollywood Musical." In *The Oxford Handbook of the Hollywood Musical,* edited by Dominic Broomfield-McHugh, 567–586. New York: Oxford University Press, 2022.

Lindeperg, Sylvie, and Bill Marshall. "Time, History and Memory in *Les Parapluies de Cherbourg.*" In *Musicals: Hollywood and Beyond,* edited by Bill Marshall and Robynn Stilwell, 98–106. Exeter: Intellect Books, 2000.

Lott, Eric. *Love and Theft: Blackface Minstrelsy and the American Working Class.* New York: Oxford University Press, 1993.

Maner, Sequoia. *To Pimp a Butterfly.* 33 1/3 Series. London: Bloomsbury, 2022.

McMillin, Scott. *The Musical as Drama.* Princeton, NJ: Princeton University Press, 2006.

Morrison, Matthew. "Race, Blacksound, and the (Re)Making of Musicological Discourse." *Journal of the American Musicological Society* 72, no. 3 (2019): 781–823.

Most, Andrea. *Making Americans: Jews and the Broadway Musical.* Cambridge, MA: Harvard University Press, 2004.

Mueller, John. *Astaire Dancing: The Musical Films*. New York: Alfred A. Knopf, 1985.

Muir, John Kenneth. *Singing a New Tune: The Rebirth of the Modern Film Musical, from "Evita" to "De-Lovely" and Beyond*. New York: Applause Theatre & Cinema Books, 2005.

Les Parapluies de Cherbourg Press File. Accessed February 21, 2023. https://www.cine-tama ris.fr/wp-content/uploads/2018/07/dossier_de_presse_les_parapluies_de_cherbourg.pdf.

Powrie, Phil, and Marie Cadalanu. *The French Film Musical*. London: Bloomsbury Academic, 2020.

Richardson, John, Claudia Gorbman, and Carol Vernallis, eds. *The Oxford Handbook of New Audiovisual Aesthetics*. New York: Oxford University Press, 2013.

Robertson, Pamela. "Feminist Camp in *Gold Diggers of 1933*." In *Hollywood Musicals: The Film Reader*, edited by Steven Cohan, 129–142. London: Routledge, 2002.

Rodosthenous, George, ed. *Twenty-First Century Musicals: From Stage to Screen*. New York: Routledge, 2018.

Rogin, Michael. *Blackface, White Noise: Jewish Immigrants in the Hollywood Melting Pot*. Berkeley: University of California Press, 1996.

Roth, Mark. "Some Warners Musicals and the Spirit of the New Deal." In *Genre: The Musical— A Reader*, edited by Rick Altman, 41–56. London: Routledge, 1981.

Rush, Adam. "Oh, What a Beautiful Mormon: Rodgers, Hammerstein, Intertextuality and *The Book of Mormon*." *Studies in Musical Theatre* 11, no. 1 (2017): 39–50.

Rush, Adam Christopher. "Recycled Culture: The Significance of Intertextuality in Twenty-First Century Musical Theatre." PhD diss., University of Lincoln, 2017.

Solis, Gabriel. "Soul, Afrofuturism & the Timeliness of Contemporary Jazz Fusions." *Dædalus* 148, no. 2 (Spring 2019): 23–35.

Stilwell, Robynn J. "Le Demy-monde: The Bewitched, Betwixt, and Between French Musical." In *Popular Music in France from* Chanson *to* Techno, edited by Hugh Dauncey and Steve Cannon, 123–138. London: Routledge, 2003.

Stilwell, Robynn J. "Theatricality, Artifice, and Affective Space in the Works of Baz Luhrmann," in *The Oxford Handbook of the Hollywood Musical*, edited by Dominic Broomfield-McHugh, 523–548. New York: Oxford University Press, 2022.

Verevis, Constantine. *Film Remakes*. Edinburgh: Edinburgh University Press, 2006.

Vernallis, Carol. "Accelerated Aesthetics: A New Lexicon of Time, Space, and Rhythm." In *The Oxford Handbook of Sound and Image in Digital Media*, edited by Carol Vernallis, John Richardson, and Amy Herzog, 707–731. New York: Oxford University Press, 2013.

Vernallis, Carol. *Experiencing Music Video: Aesthetics and Cultural Context*. New York: Columbia University Press, 2004.

Vernallis, Carol. *Unruly Media: YouTube, Music Video, and the New Digital Cinema*. New York: Oxford University Press, 2013.

Voeltz, Richard A. "'The Joke's on History': Retro-Reality, Twee, and Mediated Nostalgia in *La La Land* (2016)." *Bright Lights Film Journal*, October 13, 2018. https://brightlightsfilm. com/the-jokes-on-history-retro-reality-twee-and-mediated-nostalgia-in-la-la-land-2016/.

Williams, Alan. *Republic of Images: A History of French Filmmaking*. Cambridge, MA: Harvard University Press, 1992.

Woll, Allen. *Black Musical Theatre: From "Coontown" to "Dreamgirls."* Baton Rouge: Louisiana State University Press, 1989.

Yang, Mina. "*Moulin Rouge!* and the Undoing of Opera." *Cambridge Opera Journal* 20 (2008): 269–282.

Popular Sources

ABC News. "John Legend Reveals What Made Him Jealous of Ryan Gosling." *ABC News*, December 2, 2016, accessed December 6, 2022. https://abcnews.go.com/Entertainment/john-legend-reveals-made-jealous-ryan-gosling/story?id=43929955.

Abdul-Jabbar, Kareem. "How 'La La Land' Misleads on Race, Romance and Jazz." *The Hollywood Reporter*, February 15, 2017, accessed November 17, 2022. https://www.holly woodreporter.com/news/general-news/la-la-land-disappoints-bigoted-race-portrayal-childish-romance-975786/.

Ahmed, Tufayel. "Inside the Magic of 'La La Land' with Music Director Marius De Vries." *Newsweek*, January 4, 2017, accessed December 29, 2021. https://www.newsweek.com/inside-musical-magic-la-la-land-music-director-marius-de-vries-538510.

Artsy, Avishay. "From Vision to Reality: Landing 'La La' on the Big Screen." *Jewish Journal*, February 24, 2017, accessed December 29, 2021. https://jewishjournal.com/culture/special_sections/oscars/215553/vision-reality-landing-la-la-big-screen/.

Barna, Ben. "'La La Land' Opens the Venice Film Festival, Leaving Critics Breathless." *Nylon*, August 31, 2016, accessed November 17, 2022. https://www.nylon.com/articles/first-la-la-land-reviews.

Barnard, Linda. "John Legend on Acting for La La Land." *Toronto Star*, December 23, 2016, accessed November 2, 2022. https://www.thestar.com/entertainment/movies/2016/12/23/john-legend-on-acting-for-la-la-land.html.

Barnes, Brooks. "'La La Land' Wins Top Prize at Toronto International Film Festival." *New York Times*, September 18, 2016, accessed November 17, 2022. https://www.nytimes.com/2016/09/19/movies/la-la-land-wins-top-prize-at-toronto-international-film-festival.html.

Barnes, Brooks, and Cara Buckley. "'Moonlight,' 'La La Land' and Everything Else That Happened at the Oscars." *New York Times*, February 26, 2017, accessed November 17, 2022. https://www.nytimes.com/2017/02/26/movies/oscars-academy-awards.html.

Barnes, Brooks, and Cara Buckley. "What It Was Like Onstage during the Oscars 2017 Best Picture Mistake." *New York Times*, February 27, 2017, accessed November 17, 2022. https://www.nytimes.com/2017/02/27/movies/oscars-best-picture-moonlight-academy-awards.html.

Bradshaw, Peter. "La La Land Review: Ryan Gosling and Emma Stone Shine in a Sun-Drenched Musical Masterpiece." *Guardian*, August 31, 2016, accessed November 17, 2022. https://www.theguardian.com/film/2016/aug/31/la-la-land-review-ryan-gosling-emma-stone.

Brody, Richard. "The Empty Exertions of 'La La Land.'" *The New Yorker*, December 8, 2016, accessed November 17, 2022. https://www.newyorker.com/culture/richard-brody/the-empty-exertions-of-la-la-land.

Buchanan, Kyle, and John Horn. "The Oscars Will Be More Political Than Ever, and That's a Good Thing." *Vulture*, February 6, 2017, accessed November 17, 2022. https://www.vulture.com/2017/02/the-2017-oscars-will-be-more-political-than-ever.html.

Burr, Ty. "'La La Land' Resurrects the Classic Movie Musical." *Boston Globe*, December 14, 2016, accessed November 17, 2022. https://www.bostonglobe.com/arts/movies/2016/12/14/land-resurrects-classic-movie-musical/rpGJw3nvb3jEsK4PQAZrrK/story.html.

Calvario, Liz. "'La La Land' Composer Justin Hurwitz Breaks Down Emma Stone's Passionate 'Audition' Song." *IndieWire*, December 23, 2016, accessed December 5, 2022. https://www.indiewire.com/2016/12/la-la-land-composer-justin-hurwitz-breaks-down-emma-stone-audition-song-1201762508/.

Calvario, Liz. "'La La Land': Rostam Criticizes the Musical's Race Narrative and Lack of Queer Characters." *IndieWire*, December 21, 2016, accessed November 17, 2022. https://www.indiewire.com/2016/12/la-la-land-rostam-criticizes-film-race-narrative-lack-queer-characters-1201761773/.

Caramanica, Jon. "Does 'La La Land' Get Jazz, or Exploit It?" *New York Times*, January 25, 2017, accessed November 2, 2022. https://www.nytimes.com/2017/01/25/arts/music/la-la-land-damien-chazelle-jazz.html.

Chambers, Seve. "*La La Land* Is Clueless About What's Actually Happening in Jazz." *Vulture*, January 13, 2017, accessed November 2, 2022. https://www.vulture.com/2017/01/what-la-la-land-gets-wrong-about-todays-jazz.html.

Chinen, Nate. "The Gig: Behold the Jazzbro." *Jazz Times*, November 1, 2021, accessed November 2, 2022. https://jazztimes.com/features/columns/the-gig-behold-the-jazzbro/.

Chow, Andrew R. "How 3 Key *In the Heights* Scenes Were Reimagined from Stage to Screen." *Time*, June 15, 2021, accessed March 8, 2022. https://time.com/6072445/in-the-heights-stage-screen/.

Cine Extras. "La La Land 2016—Behind the Scenes—Ryan Gosling: Piano Student." *YouTube*, May 23, 2020, accessed December 6, 2022. https://www.youtube.com/watch?v=rjz6 7NtbzQk.

Cunningham, Malorie. "The Making of 'La La Land': Why It's Important to Modern Cinema." *ABC News*, February 21, 2017, accessed March 8, 2022. https://abcnews.go.com/Entertainment/making-la-la-land-important-modern-cinema/story?id=45112391.

Dabrowska, Diana. "La La Land (Damien Chazelle, US)—Special Presentations." *Cinema Scope*, 2016, accessed February 23, 2022. https://cinema-scope.com/cinema-scope-online/la-la-land-damien-chazelle-us-special-presentations/.

Dargis, Manohla. "'La La Land' Makes Musicals Matter Again." *New York Times*, November 23, 2016, accessed December 8, 2022. https://www.nytimes.com/2016/11/23/movies/la-la-land-makes-musicals-matter-again.html.

Dargis, Manohla, and A. O. Scott. "The 25 Best Films of the 21st Century So Far." *The New York Times*, June 9, 2017, accessed November 17, 2022. https://www.nytimes.com/interactive/2017/06/09/movies/the-25-best-films-of-the-21st-century.html.

Davies, Morgan Leigh. "Art in the Age of Masculinist Hollywood: Damien Chazelle's 'La La Land.'" *Los Angeles Review of Books*, January 2, 2017, accessed November 17, 2022. https://lareviewofbooks.org/article/art-age-masculinist-hollywood-damien-chazelles-la-la-land/.

Desta, Yohana. "*La La Land* Stuns at the Venice Film Festival." *Vanity Fair*, August 31, 2016, accessed November 17, 2022. https://www.vanityfair.com/hollywood/2016/08/la-la-land-venice-reviews.

De Vries, Marius, and Clarisse Loughrey. "La La Land: Here's a Track-by-Track Breakdown of the Soundtrack by the Film's Music Director." *Independent*, February 9, 2017, accessed December 29, 2021. https://www.independent.co.uk/arts-entertainment/films/features/la-la-land-soundtrack-oscars-2017-city-of-stars-another-day-of-sun-audition-a7571571.html.

Dowd, A. A. "*Whiplash* Maestro Damien Chazelle on Drumming, Directing, and J. K. Simmons." *AV Club*, October 15, 2014, accessed December 29, 2021. https://www.avclub.com/whiplash-maestro-damien-chazelle-on-drumming-directing-1798273033.

Easter, Makeda. "'La La Land's' Creative Team Goes Behind the Scenes of the Ryan Gosling, Emma Stone Musical." *Los Angeles Times*, December 11, 2016, accessed December 29, 2021. https://www.latimes.com/entertainment/movies/moviesnow/la-et-mn-la-la-land-panel-20161211-story.html.

Eyewitness News. "'Moonlight' or 'La La Land'? Best Picture Mix-up at Oscars." *YouTube*, February 27, 2017, accessed November 17, 2022. https://www.youtube.com/watch?v=8KeOxeuiZjs.

Feinberg, Scott. "Telluride: 'La La Land' Opens to Big Applause; Could Extend Fest's Oscar Streak (Analysis)." *Hollywood Reporter*, September 2, 2016, accessed November 17, 2022. https://www.hollywoodreporter.com/news/general-news/la-la-land-opens-telluride-925519/.

Fleming, Mike Jr. "No. 18 'La La Land' Box Office Profits—2016 Most Valuable Movie Blockbuster Tournament." *Deadline*, March 21, 2017, accessed November 17, 2022. https://deadline.com/2017/03/la-la-land-box-office-profit-2016-1202047487/.

Ford, Rebecca. "How 'La La Land' Went from First-Screening Stumbles to Hollywood Ending." *The Hollywood Reporter*, November 3, 2016, accessed December 29, 2021. https://www.hollywoodreporter.com/movies/movie-features/la-la-land-unrealistic-hollywood-dream-critical-acclaim-942793/.

Ford, Rebecca. "Oscars: 'La La Land' Producer on Making a Pact to Never Change the Film's Ending." *Hollywood Reporter*, February 12, 2017, accessed December 29, 2021. https://www.hollywoodreporter.com/movies/movie-news/oscars-la-la-land-producer-making-a-pact-never-change-films-ending-973909/.

Framke, Caroline. "Emma Stone's La La Land Performance Transcends the Film's Biggest Flaw: A Poorly Written Female Lead." *Vox*, February 27, 2017, accessed March 2, 2023. https://www.vox.com/culture/2017/1/5/14153546/emma-stone-la-la-land-best-actress.

France, Lisa Respers. "Oscar Mistake Overshadows Historic Moment for 'Moonlight.'" *CNN Entertainment*, February 28, 2017, accessed November 17, 2022. https://www.cnn.com/2017/02/27/entertainment/moonlight-oscars-win/index.html.

Fung, Lisa. "For Choreographer Mandy Moore, 'La La Land' Was 'the Super Bowl of My Career.'" *Los Angeles Times*, December 29, 2016, accessed December 29, 2021. https://www.latimes.com/entertainment/envelope/la-en-mn-1229-mandy-moore-20161228-story.html.

Galuppo, Mia. "'La La Land' to Become a Broadway Musical." *Hollywood Reporter*, February 7, 2023, accessed March 2, 2023. https://www.hollywoodreporter.com/lifestyle/arts/la-la-land-broadway-musical-1235319367/.

Garrett, Diane. "'La La Land' Refurbished the Classic Musical Format for a Modern Audience." *Variety*, February 16, 2017, accessed February 23, 2022. https://variety.com/2017/film/awards/la-la-land-revives-musical-genre-1201989409/.

Gleiberman, Owen. "Film Review: 'La La Land,'" *Variety*, August 31, 2016, accessed November 17, 2022. https://variety.com/2016/film/reviews/la-la-land-review-venice-ryan-gosling-emma-stone-1201846576/.

Go Creative Show. "'When the Sun Goes Down' Breakdown—IN THE HEIGHTS (Show Short)." *YouTube*, July 1, 2021, accessed March 8, 2022. https://www.youtube.com/watch?v=o1MFgYPDgCM.

Graham, David A. "Jazzbros: A Force for Jazzgood or Jazzevil?" *Atlantic*, August 15, 2013, accessed November 2, 2022. https://www.theatlantic.com/entertainment/archive/2013/08/jazzbros-a-force-for-jazzgood-or-jazzevil/278696/.

Hammond, Pete. "Damien Chazelle's 'La La Land,' an Ode to Musicals, Romance & L.A., Ready to Launch Venice and Oscar Season." *Deadline*, August 30, 2016, accessed December 29, 2021. https://deadline.com/2016/08/damien-chazelle-la-la-land-venice-film-festival-1201810810/.

Hammond, Pete. "'La La Land' Review: A Gorgeous Musical Romance for This Age—And the Ages." *Deadline*, December 9, 2016 [originally published August 31, 2016], accessed November 17, 2022. https://deadline.com/2016/12/la-la-land-review-emma-stone-ryan-gosling-damien-chazelle-video-1201811177/.

Harris, Aisha. "*La La Land*'s Many References to Classic Movies: A Guide." *Slate*, December 13, 2016, accessed March 1, 2022. https://slate.com/culture/2016/12/la-la-lands-many-references-to-classic-movies-from-singin-in-the-rain-to-the-red-balloon-to-funny-face.html.

Hautman, Nicholas. "Jordan Horowitz: 5 Things to Know About the 'La La Land' Producer Who Graciously Cleared Up #EnvelopeGate." *US Weekly*, February 27, 2017, accessed December 29, 2021. https://www.usmagazine.com/entertainment/news/jordan-horowitz-5-things-to-know-about-the-la-la-land-producer-w469355/.

Hipes, Patrick. "'La La Land' Added as AFI Fest Centerpiece Gala." *Deadline*, October 20, 2016, accessed November 17, 2022. https://deadline.com/2016/10/la-la-land-afi-fest-2016-centerpiece-gala-1201839999/.

Hipes, Patrick, and Dominic Patten. "Ryan Gosling & Emma Stone Circling Damien Chazelle's 'La La Land.'" *Deadline*, April 14, 2015, accessed December 29, 2021. https://deadline.com/2015/04/ryan-gosling-emma-stone-damien-chazelle-la-la-land-1201409697/.

Hobbs, Thomas. "The History of the West Coast Get Down, LA's Jazz Giants." *Dazed*, June 26, 2020, accessed November 2, 2022. https://www.dazeddigital.com/music/article/49630/1/west-coast-get-down-los-angeles-jazz-collective-interview.

Hopewell, John. "Ryan Gosling, Emma Stone, Damien Chazelle's 'La La Land' Wow Venice." *Variety*, August 31, 2016, accessed November 17, 2022. https://variety.com/2016/film/festivals/ryan-gosling-emma-stone-la-la-land-wow-venice-1201848676/.

"How *La La Land* Pulled Off That Stunning Highway Dance Sequence." *Vanity Fair*, April 25, 2017, accessed March 8, 2022. https://www.vanityfair.com/hollywood/2017/04/la-la-land-another-day-of-sun-song-video.

Howard, Annie. "'La La Land' Producer Marc Platt on Damien Chazelle's Love of Filmmaking." *Hollywood Reporter*, November 5, 2016, accessed December 29, 2021. https://www.hollywoodreporter.com/movies/movie-news/la-la-land-producer-marc-platt-damien-chazelles-love-filmmaking-oscar-producer-roundtable-94432-944322/.

Hyfler, Richard. "Whiplash, or the Limits of Abuse." *Forbes*, January 8, 2015, accessed July 15, 2022. https://www.forbes.com/sites/richardhyfler/2015/01/08/whiplash-or-the-limits-of-abuse/.

Izundu, Chi Chi. "Oscars So White: What People Are Saying About Diversity in Hollywood." *BBC News*, January 19, 2016, accessed November 17, 2022. https://www.bbc.com/news/newsbeat-35349772.

Jordan, Leila. "*Moonlight, La La Land*, and the 2017 Best Picture Oscars Flub, Five Years Later." *Paste Magazine*, February 26, 2022, accessed November 17, 2022. https://www.pastemagazine.com/movies/moonlight-la-la-land-oscars-error-legacy/.

Keller, Louise. "La La Land." *Urban Cinefile*, accessed December 5, 2022. https://web.archive.org/web/20170217151824/urbancinefile.com.au/home/view.asp?a=21959&s=Reviews.

Kim, Eunice Y. "Student Work Featured at NYC Tribeca Film Festival." *Harvard Crimson*, April 24, 2009, accessed December 29, 2021. https://www.thecrimson.com/article/2009/4/24/student-work-featured-at-nyc-tribeca/.

"'La La Land' High-Flying Highway Opening Scene: How'd They Do That?" *The Wrap*, December 9, 2016, accessed March 8, 2022. https://www.thewrap.com/la-la-land-opening-scene-how-they-do-that/.

"'La La Land' to Centerpiece Middleburg Film Festival." *Middleburg Life*, accessed November 17, 2022. https://www.middleburglife.com/20161013la-la-land-to-centerpiece-middlburg-film-festival/.

Lane, Anthony. "Fun in 'La La Land.'" *New Yorker*, December 4, 2016, accessed November 17, 2022. https://www.newyorker.com/magazine/2016/12/12/dancing-with-the-stars.

LaSalle, Mick. "Beautiful, Hopeful 'La La Land' Is One of the Year's Best." *SF Gate*, December 9, 2016, accessed November 17, 2022. https://www.sfgate.com/movies/article/Beautiful-hopeful-La-La-Land-is-one-of-the-10786350.php.

Lawler, Kelly. "Oscar Nominations 2017: The Case against 'La La Land.'" *USA Today*, January 11, 2017, accessed November 17, 2022. https://www.usatoday.com/story/life/movies/2017/01/11/la-la-land-golden-globes-backlash/96360032/.

Lawson, Richard. "*La La Land* Is a Wonder, and Another Big Breakthrough for Emma Stone." *Vanity Fair*, September 3, 2016, accessed November 17, 2022. https://www.vanityfair.com/hollywood/2016/09/la-la-land-review.

Lincoln, Kevin. "For the *La La Land* Lyricists, Getting Hired Was Like Looking in the Mirror." *Vulture*, January 5, 2017, accessed December 29, 2021. https://www.vulture.com/2016/12/pasek-paul-la-la-land-songwriters.html.

Lincoln, Kevin. "What You Should Know About Damien Chazelle's Little-Seen First Film, *Guy and Madeline on a Park Bench*." *Vulture*, January 9, 2017, accessed December 29, 2021. https://www.vulture.com/2017/01/damien-chazelle-first-film-guy-and-madeline-park-bench.html.

Lind, Abigail, and Rebecca A. Schuetz. "The Scenic Route: Harvard Filmmaking Flourishes Despite Industry Troubles." *Harvard Crimson*, February 23, 2010, accessed December 29, 2021. https://www.thecrimson.com/article/2010/2/23/the-scenic-route/.

Lott-Lavigna, Ruby. "La La Land Review: An Ambitious Musical Soured by Racist Undertones." *Wired*, October 1, 2016, accessed November 17, 2022. https://www.wired.co.uk/article/la-la-land-trailer-review.

"Love 'La La Land'? Hate It? So Do We." *New York Times*, February 15, 2017, accessed November 17, 2022. https://www.nytimes.com/2017/02/15/movies/la-la-land-love-hate.html.

Macdonald, Moira. "'La La Land' Review: Get Lost in This Dreamy Musical." *Seattle Times*, December 13, 2016, accessed November 17, 2022. https://www.seattletimes.com/entertainment/movies/la-la-land-review-get-lost-in-this-dreamy-musical/.

Madison, Ira III. "'La La Land''s White Jazz Narrative." *MTV.com*, December 19, 2016, accessed November 2, 2022. http://www.mtv.com/news/2965622/la-la-lands-white-jazz-narrative/.

Marchese, David. "*La La Land* Director Damien Chazelle Breaks Down Jazz's Popularity Problem." *Vulture*, December 19, 2016, accessed December 7, 2022. https://www.vulture.com/2016/12/la-la-land-damien-chazelle-jazz-nostalgia.html.

McCarthy, Todd. "'La La Land': Venice Review." *Hollywood Reporter*, August 31, 2016, accessed November 17, 2022. https://www.hollywoodreporter.com/news/general-news/la-la-land-review-emma-stone-ryan-gosling-924458/.

Morris, Wesley. "Movie Review: Guy and Madeline on a Park Bench." *Boston Globe*, December 17, 2010, accessed December 29, 2021. http://archive.boston.com/ae/movies/articles/2010/12/17/a_boston_movie_that_plays_a_different_tune/.

Nelson, Geoff. "The Unbearable Whiteness of *La La Land*." *Paste Magazine*, January 6, 2017, accessed February 23, 2022. https://www.pastemagazine.com/movies/la-la-land/the-unbearable-whiteness-of-la-la-land/.

Nerdwriter1. "Intertextuality: Hollywood's New Currency." *YouTube*, May 25, 2016, accessed February 23, 2022. https://www.youtube.com/watch?v=QeAKX_0wZWY.

Newman, Melinda. "John Legend on Producing & Acting in 'La La Land,' Broadway Plans, 'Role Model' Quincy Jones." *Billboard*, January 6, 2017, accessed November 2, 2022. https://www.billboard.com/articles/news/7647809/john-legend-la-la-land-broadway-quincy-jones.

Nicholson, Amy. "'La La Land': A City of Tap-Dancing Angels." *MTV.com*, December 7, 2016, accessed January 30, 2023. https://www.mtv.com/news/kwl7m5/la-la-lands-emma-stone-ryan-gosling-review.

Nolfi, Joey. "Telluride Film Festival: Tom Hanks Interrupts Sully Q&A to Praise La La Land." *EW*, September 4, 2016, accessed November 17, 2022. https://ew.com/article/2016/09/04/telluride-tom-hanks-praises-la-la-land/.

O'Falt, Chris. "'In the Heights': How They Danced Up the Side of a Building." *IndieWire*, June 18, 2021, accessed March 8, 2021. https://www.indiewire.com/2021/06/in-the-heights-behind-the-scenes-dance-up-side-of-building-1234645393/.

Olcese, Abby. "'La La Land' Is Dreamy, but a Film in the Wrong Year." *Sojourners*, December 14, 2016, accessed November 17, 2022. https://sojo.net/articles/la-la-land-dreamy-film-wrong-year.

Orr, Christopher. "The Novelty and Nostalgia of *La La Land*." *Atlantic*, December 9, 2016, accessed November 17, 2022. https://www.theatlantic.com/entertainment/archive/2016/12/la-la-land-review-damien-chazelle-ryan-gosling-emma-stone/510092/.

Piccini, Sara. "The Greatest Showmen." *W&M Alumni Magazine*, January 7, 2020, accessed March 8, 2022. https://magazine.wm.edu/issue/2020-winter/the-greatest-showmen.php.

Preciado, Sara. "La La Land—Movie References." *YouTube*, January 22, 2017, accessed February 23, 2022. https://www.youtube.com/watch?v=iI5BPRrj554.

Radish, Christina. "'La La Land' Writer/Director Damien Chazelle on Reviving 'Old Hollywood' Techniques." *Collider*, December 9, 2016, accessed December 29, 2021. https://collider.com/la-la-land-damien-chazelle-interview/.

Ratliff, Ben. "Jazz Hate: *La La Land* May Be a Great Movie About Dreams, but as a Movie About Jazz, It's a Muddle of Clichés." *Slate*, December 15, 2016, accessed November 2, 2022. https://slate.com/culture/2016/12/la-la-lands-cliched-confused-depiction-of-jazz.html.

Reed, Rex. "Good-Intentioned but Overrated, 'La La Land' Reeks of Mothballs." *Observer*, December 15, 2016, accessed November 17, 2022. https://observer.com/2016/12/good-intentioned-but-overrated-la-la-land-reeks-of-mothballs/.

Rees, Jaspar. "Interview: Marius de Vries, Musical Director of *La La Land*." *Theartsdesk.com*, January 14, 2017, accessed December 29, 2021. https://theartsdesk.com/film/interview-marius-de-vries-musical-director-la-la-land.

Riley, Jenelle. "'La La Land': Ryan Gosling and Emma Stone on Dancing through Their Third Onscreen Romance." *Variety*, November 15, 2016, accessed November 2, 2022. https://variety.com/2016/film/features/la-la-land-ryan-gosling-emma-stone-damien-chazelle-1201917796/.

Robinette, Dale. "'La La Land': Go Inside the Epilogue." *USA Today*, February 21, 2017, accessed February 23, 2022. https://www.usatoday.com/picture-gallery/life/movies/2017/02/17/la-la-land-go-inside-the-epilogue/98073462/.

Roschke, Ryan. "John Legend Laughed at Me When I Asked If Ryan Gosling Came to Him for Piano Tips." *Pop Sugar*, January 31, 2017, accessed December 7, 2022. https://www.popsugar.com/entertainment/John-Legend-Interview-About-La-La-Land-January-2017-43080913.

Roschke, Ryan. "Singin' in the Rain Impacted La La Land More Than You Think." *Pop Sugar*, February 23, 2017, accessed February 23, 2022. https://www.popsugar.com/entertainment/La-La-Land-Inspired-Singin-Rain-43061632.

Saturday Night Live. "La La Land Interrogation—SNL." *YouTube*, January 22, 2017, accessed November 17, 2022. https://www.youtube.com/watch?v=abn6cPxrc5w.

Schmidlin, Charlie. "Interview: Director Damien Chazelle Talks 'Whiplash,' Musical Editing & His 'MGM-Style' Musical 'La La Land.'" *IndieWire*, October 10, 2014, accessed December 29, 2021. https://www.indiewire.com/2014/10/interview-director-damien-chazelle-talks-whiplash-musical-editing-his-mgm-style-musical-la-la-land-271422/.

Scott, A. O. "Cinema Is Dead? Telluride Says Not Yet." *New York Times*, September 5, 2016, accessed November 17, 2022. https://www.nytimes.com/2016/09/06/movies/telluride-film-festival.html.

Scott, A. O. "Review: Ryan Gosling and Emma Stone Aswirl in Tra La La Land." *New York Times*, December 8, 2016, accessed February 23, 2022. https://www.nytimes.com/2016/12/08/movies/la-la-land-review-ryan-gosling-emma-stone.html.

"Shot in CinemaScope, La La Land Vibrantly Romances the Olden Days of Hollywood." Eastman Kodak, January 10, 2017, accessed March 8, 2022. https://web.archive.org/web/20170131193001/http:/motion.kodak.com/kodakgcg/us/en/motion/blog/blog_post/?contentid=4295000679.

Silman, Anna. "*La La Land*: A Musical Ode to Men Who Love Loving Jazz." *The Cut*, December 13, 2016, accessed November 17, 2022. https://www.thecut.com/2016/12/la-la-land-two-hours-of-ryan-gosling-explaining-jazz.html.

Sims, David. "The Lead Contenders for This Year's Oscars." *Atlantic*, December 8, 2016, accessed November 17, 2022. https://www.theatlantic.com/entertainment/archive/2016/12/oscars-2017-favorites-la-la-land-moonlight/509864/.

Tate, Greg. "Why Jazz Will Always Be Relevant." *Fader*, May 5, 2016, accessed November 2, 2022. http://www.thefader.com/2016/05/05/jazz-will-always-be-relevant.

Tingen, Paul. "Inside Track: *La La Land*. Secrets of the Mix Engineers: Marius de Vries & Nicholai Baxter." *Sound on Sound*, April 2017, accessed December 29, 2021. https://www.soundonsound.com/techniques/inside-track-la-la-land.

"Tribeca '09 Interview: 'Guy and Madeline on a Park Bench' Director Damien Chazelle." *IndieWire*, April 17, 2009, accessed December 29, 2021. https://www.indiewire.com/2009/

04/tribeca-09-interview-guy-and-madeline-on-a-park-bench-director-damien-chazelle-70645/.

Truitt, Brian. "Review: Prepare to Be Enchanted by Magical Musical 'La La Land.'" *USA Today*, December 5, 2016, accessed November 17, 2022. https://www.usatoday.com/story/life/movies/2016/12/05/review-la-la-land-movie/94790704/.

Ugwu, Reggie. "The Hashtag That Changed the Oscars: An Oral History," *New York Times*, February 6, 2020, accessed November 17, 2022. https://www.nytimes.com/2020/02/06/movies/oscarssowhite-history.html.

Vivarelli, Nick. "'La La Land' Opens 73rd Venice Film Festival on Upbeat Note Despite Tight Security." *Variety*, August 31, 2016, accessed November 17, 2022. https://variety.com/2016/film/festivals/venice-film-festival-2016-opening-ceremony-la-la-land-1201849005/.

Walls, Seth Colter. "Is Jazz Entering a New Golden Age?" *Guardian*, July 8, 2016, accessed November 2, 2022. https://www.theguardian.com/music/2016/jul/08/is-jazz-entering-a-new-golden-age.

Watkins, Gwynne. "Oscar Frontrunner 'La La Land' Is a Good Movie, but a Bad Musical." *Yahoo! Entertainment*, January 24, 2017, accessed January 30, 2023. https://www.yahoo.com/entertainment/oscar-front-runner-la-la-land-is-a-good-movie-but-a-bad-musical-192724174.html.

Wilkinson, Alissa. "La La Land Sees Old Hollywood Magic Giving Way to Modern Melancholy." *Vox*, December 29, 2016, accessed February 23, 2022. https://www.vox.com/culture/2016/12/7/13868628/la-la-land-review-emma-stone-ryan-gosling-damien-chazelle.

Williams, Kam. "John Legend—Legend in La La Land!" *Philadelphia Sunday Sun*, December 15, 2016, accessed November 2, 2022. https://www.philasun.com/entertainment/john-legend-legend-la-la-land/.

Willmore, Alison. "The Privilege of Hollywood Nostalgia." *BuzzFeed*, December 20, 2016, accessed November 17, 2022. https://www.buzzfeed.com/alisonwillmore/la-la-land-and-the-privilege-of-nostalgia.

Wilson, David McKay. "The Man Behind the La La Magic." *Pennsylvania Gazette*, June 29, 2017, accessed December 29, 2021. https://thepenngazette.com/the-man-behind-the-la-la-magic/.

Yahr, Emily. "Your Guide to the 'La La Land' Backlash." *Washington Post*, January 25, 2017, accessed November 17, 2022. https://www.washingtonpost.com/news/arts-and-entertainment/wp/2017/01/25/your-guide-to-the-la-la-land-backlash/.

Yuan, Jada. "Toronto: Emma Stone and Ryan Gosling's *La La Land* Is the Big Beating Heart of a Movie Musical We've Been Craving." *Vulture*, September 14, 2016, accessed November 17, 2022. https://www.vulture.com/2016/09/la-la-land-charms-tiff-emma-stone-ryan-gosling.html.

Zacharek, Stephanie. "Do You Hate Musicals? The Dazzling *La La Land* Could Change That." *Time*, August 31, 2016, accessed November 17, 2022. https://time.com/4474968/la-la-land-venice-film-festival/.

Zeitchik, Steven. "Toronto 2016: 'La La Land,' Starring Ryan Gosling and Emma Stone, Is the Fest's Big Award Winner." *Los Angeles Times*, September 18, 2016, accessed November 17, 2022. https://www.latimes.com/entertainment/movies/la-et-mn-la-la-land-toronto-award-gosling-stone-chazelle-20160918-snap-story.html.

Index

For the benefit of digital users, indexed terms that span two pages (e.g., 52–53) may, on occasion, appear on only one of those pages.

Figures, examples, and tables are indicated by an italic *f*, *e*, and *t* following the page number.

Abdul-Jabbar, Kareem, 106–7
Academy Awards, 2017, 1–2, 99–100, 108–11, 110*f*
Altman, Rick, 36, 39
American in Paris, An (1951), 56–58, 89
Anchors Aweigh (1945), 65
animated musicals. *See* Disney
"Another Day of Sun"
   audience reactions to, 2, 101, 102
   in the film's development, 26–28
   overview of, 2–3, 4*t*
   parodied on *Crazy Ex-Girlfriend*, 113–14
   referenced in the Epilogue, 57
   references in, 42, 43–47, 46*f*, 70–71
   themes of, 2–3, 43–45, 46–48
   virtuosic camera in, 70–71, 72*f*
Ansari, Aziz, 99, 100*f*
Astaire, Fred
   cinematography in the films of, 65, 69, 71, 76
   Gosling compared to, 101–2
   referenced in *La La Land*, 30, 51–52, 53*f*
   relationship to Black music and dance, 88–89
"Audition (The Fools Who Dream)," 4*t*, 6, 71–74, 74*f*
auteurism, 6–7, 10–11, 16, 24–26, 32–33

Babes in Arms (1939), 87–88
Babylon (2022), 9–10
backstage musical ("show musical"), 9, 39–40, 117n.1
Ballon rouge, Le (1956), 57–58
Band Wagon, The (1953), 52, 53*f*, 57–58
Barnes, Brooks, 111
Beatty, Warren, 1, 110
Belle of New York, The (1952), 65, 71
Berger, Fred, 19, 22–23, 110, 118nn.33–34
Berkeley, Busby, 50, 70–71, 77–78
blackface, 87–89
Bordwell, David, 67–68, 70
Boym, Svetlana, 30–31
Bradshaw, Peter, 101–2

bricolage, 39–40
Broadway Melody of 1940 (1940), 57–58
Brody, Richard, 108
Brooks, Alice, 76
Buckley, Cara, 111
Burr, Ty, 106

camerawork. *See* cinematography; virtuosic camera
Carew, Anthony, 30–31
CGI (computer-generated imagery), 67–68, 70, 71, 76, 77–78
Chambers, Seve, 81–82, 95
Charisse, Cyd, 52, 53*f*, 101–2
Chazelle, Damien
   auteurist tendencies of, 10–11, 16, 24–26
   background of, 11, 12–14
   career of, 9–11, 28–29
   casting *La La Land*, 22–23, 64, 84, 90–91, 122n.14
   centrality of jazz to, 6–7, 80–81, 83
   collaborative process with Hurwitz, 15
   criticism of, 107–8
   on the Epilogue, 56–57, 58–59
   on film musicals, 11, 13–14, 40–41, 82–83
   on French film, 40–41
   at Harvard, 12–14, 117–18n.20
   on Hurwitz's music, 48
   influences on, 11–12, 40–41, 43
   interest in jazz, 79
   on intertextuality, 34–35
   on jazz in *La La Land*, 80–81
   on Keith's character, 90–91
   on *La La Land*'s cinematography, 69–70, 121n.27
   on *La La Land*'s musical numbers, 74
   on *La La Land*'s musical style, 35
   meeting Hurwitz, 12–13
   move to Hollywood, 18–19
   on the opening of *La La Land*, 27–28, 45, 48

Chazelle, Damien (*cont.*)
  on realism, 63–64
  on Sebastian's character, 82–84, 91
  style of, 14–16, 42, 43, 62
  working with Moore, 22
  working with the cast of *La La Land*, 23–24,
    56
  See also Guy and Madeline on a Park Bench
    (2009); *La La Land* (2016); *Whiplash*
    (2014)
Chicago (2002), 66–67
Chinen, Nate, 81–82
choreography, 22, 23, 45–46, 51–52, 70–71,
    88–89, 93–95
  See also Moore, Mandy; virtuosity, human
Chu, John, 76
Cinelu, Angelique, 92, 93
CinemaScope, 16, 69, 76–77
cinematography
  in the contemporary film musical, 67–68,
    74–77
  in *La La Land*, 27, 61–62, 69–74, 76–77
"City of Stars," 3, 4*t*, 21, 24, 39–40, 52–54, 55*e*
"City of Stars" Reprise, 3–6, 5*t*, 27–28, 55–56
classic Hollywood. *See* Golden Age film
    musicals
Clover, Carol, 89
Coen brothers, 32–33, 114
Cohan, Steven, 38–39
collaboration, 6–7, 9–11, 12–13, 15, 20–26,
    28–29, 92–93
conditional love songs, 51–52
Crazy Ex-Girlfriend (2015–2019), 113–14

Dabrowska, Diana, 38–39
dancing. *See* choreography
Dargis, Manohla, 103, 106
Davies, Morgan Leigh, 105, 108
de Mille, Agnes, 56–57
de Vries, Marius, 20–21, 24, 26–27, 92, 93
Decker, Todd, 87, 88–89
Demoiselles de Rochefort, Les (1967), 11–12, 40,
    41–43, 44*e*, 45–46, 46*f*
Demy, Jacques, 11–12, 13, 14, 31, 40–43, 101–2
  See also *Demoiselles de Rochefort, Les*
    (1967); *Parapluies de Cherbourg, Les*
    (1964)
Disney, 21, 26–27, 32, 66–67
dream ballets, 56–59, 121n.51
  See also "Epilogue"
dual-focus narrative, 36–38
Dunaway, Faye, 1, 110
Dyer, Richard, 77–78

Easter Parade (1948), 88–89
Efron, Zac, 75
"Epilogue," 5*t*, 6, 56–59
escapism, 30, 59–60, 103–4
  See also nostalgia

Feuer, Jane, 39, 65
film musical genre
  after the Golden Age, 66
  audiovisual syntax of, 76–78
  Black performers sidelined in, 60, 87–89, 106
  dual-focus narrative in, 36
  jazz in, 80–81, 87–88
  La La Land's potential impact on, 114
  racial masquerading in, 80, 87–89, 107
  and realism, 64, 66, 67
  referenced in *La La Land*, 30–31, 33–34,
    51–52, 59, 60
  reflexivity in, 31–32, 39–40
  reinterpreted in Demy's films, 11–12, 31
  resurgence of, 6–8, 18, 66–68
  technology in, 64–65
  See also Golden Age film musicals;
    intertextuality; nostalgia
film technology, 31–32, 62, 64–65, 67–68, 69–71
  See also CGI (computer-generated imagery);
    virtuosic camera
First Man (2018), 9–10
Flying Lotus, 96, 97
Focus Features, 18–19
French New Wave, 11–12, 32–33, 40–42
  See also Demy, Jacques
Funny Face (1957), 57–58

Gabbard, Krin, 85–86, 88
Garcia, Desirée, 16, 30, 84
Garland, Judy, 64–65, 87–88
Garrett, Diane, 59
Gleiberman, Owen, 101
Godard, Jean-Luc, 11–12, 32–33
Golden Age film musicals
  nostalgia for, 1–2, 6–7, 30–32, 33–35, 67
  parodies of, 114
  performers' virtuosity foregrounded in,
    64–65
  reflexivity in, 39–40
  See also film musical genre
Gosling, Ryan
  critics on, 63, 101–2, 105–6
  in *La La Land*'s development process, 22–24,
    27–28, 56, 64, 119n.54
  performance by, 63, 64, 91
  See also La La Land (2016)

Gracey, Michael, 74–75
Graham, David A., 82, 89–90
Great American Songbook, 35, 80–81
Greatest Showman, The (2017), 21, 66–67,
    74–75, 114
Guy and Madeline on a Park Bench (2009)
    compared to *La La Land*, 14–15, 16, 23–24,
        28–29
    filmmaking process for, 13–16, 23–24
    "Love in the Fall," 15–16, 16*e*, 17*f*
    music reused in *La La Land*, 45, 85–86
    as precursor to *La La Land*, 6–7, 13–16,
        58–59

Hammond, Pete, 101–2
Hanks, Tom, 102
Harvard University, 9, 11, 12–14, 117–18n.20
"Herman's Habit," 3, 4*t*, 15–16, 84, 85*f*
Hollywood film musicals. *See* film musical
    genre; Golden Age film musicals
Horowitz, Jordan, 19, 22, 110*f*, 110, 118n.33
Howland, John, 13
Hurwitz, Justin
    background of, 12–13
    career of, 9–11, 28–29
    on "City of Stars," 54, 120n.48
    collaboration on "Start a Fire," 92, 93
    collaborative process with Chazelle, 15
    at Harvard, 12–14
    influences on, 13, 40, 43
    on jazz, 12, 83
    on Legrand's music, 43
    meeting Chazelle, 12–13
    move to Hollywood, 18–19
    on music theory, 12, 48
    on the opening of *La La Land*, 27–28
    orchestrations for *La La Land*, 26–27
    style of, 14–16, 35, 48
    tension with Lionsgate and Interscope, 26–27
    working with Pasek and Paul, 21–22
    working with the cast of *La La Land*, 24
    See also Guy and Madeline on a Park Bench
        (2009); *La La Land* (2016); *Whiplash*
        (2014)

In the Heights (2021), 76, 114
Interscope, 26
intertextuality
    in "Another Day of Sun," 42, 43–47, 46*f*,
        70–71
    as central to *La La Land*, 6–7, 30–31, 33–35,
        59–60
    in "City of Stars," 54

in contemporary cinema, 32–33
definition of, 32
in Demy's films, 11–12, 31, 40, 41–42, 43
in the Epilogue, 56–58
in *La La Land* with Demy's films, 40, 42–43
in "A Lovely Night," 51–52, 53*f*
in musical theater, 32
and nostalgia, 1–2, 6–7, 33–35, 44–45, 60
in "Someone in the Crowd," 43–44, 49–50, 50*f*
and the viewing experience, 2, 59–60

Jackman, Hugh, 75
jazz
    ambivalence about, 7, 80, 83
    as central to *La La Land*, 7, 79–81
    contemporary scene, 96–97
    discourse on, 81–82
    in film musicals, 80–81, 87–88
    in *Guy and Madeline on a Park Bench*, 14–16,
        79
    Hurwitz's interest in, 12
    "jazzbro" stereotype, 82–84
    and nostalgia, 79–81, 83, 97–98
    Sebastian's view of, 7, 37, 79–80, 81–84, 89–
        90, 95, 97–98
    in *Whiplash*, 19–20, 79
    and whiteness, 7, 79–80, 83–90, 97, 106–7,
        122n.15
Jazz Singer, The (1927), 87–88
Jolson, Al, 87–88
Jordan, Leila, 111
jukebox musicals, 32, 66–67

Keller, Louise, 59
Kelly, Gene
    cinematography in the films of, 64–65, 69
    referenced in *La La Land*, 30, 51, 56–57
    relationship to Black music and dance, 88–89
    See also Singin' in the Rain (1952)
Kessler, Kelly, 66
King, Geoff, 67–68
King of Jazz (1930), 88
Knapp, Raymond, 66

La La Land (2016)
    absence of contemporary jazz from, 95–97
    ambivalence about nostalgia in, 30–31, 33–
        34, 47, 58–59, 60, 78
    awards and nominations, 1–2, 9, 102–3, 104,
        108–10
    backlash to, 7, 99–100, 104–8, 111–12
    Broadway adaptation of (forthcoming), 114,
        124n.1

La La Land (2016) (*cont.*)
  casting of, 22–23, 84
  centrality of jazz to, 7, 79–81, 83, 97–98
  cinematography of, 27, 61–62, 69–74,
    76–77
  compared to *Guy and Madeline on a Park
    Bench*, 14–15, 16, 23–24, 28–29
  cultural impact of, 7–8, 111–12,
    113–15
  cynicism in, 30, 31, 33–34, 47–48, 50
  development of, 10–11, 20–28
  dual-focus narrative in, 36–38
  early concepts for, 18–19
  at film festivals, 101–3
  gender politics of, 106, 107–8
  influence of Demy on, 40–43
  intertextuality as central to, 6–7, 30–31, 33–
    35, 59–60
  musical numbers (overview), 2–6, 4t–5t
  Oscars mix-up, 1–2, 99–100, 108–11, 110f
  parodied on *Crazy Ex-Girlfriend*, 113–14
  plot summary, 2–6, 36–39
  praise for, 1–2, 99, 101–4
  racial representation in, 83–86, 89–90, 92, 95,
    98, 99, 106–7
  as "realist musical," 61–64, 71–74, 76–77
  studio interest in producing, 19, 20
  "timeless" musical style of, 35
  whiteness and jazz in, 7, 79–80, 83–87, 89–
    90, 97, 106–7, 122n.15
  See also reception of *La La Land*
"La La Land" (cut song), 27–28, 56
Lamar, Kendrick, 96
Lane, Anthony, 103–4
LaSalle, Mick, 103–4
Lawler, Kelly, 105
Legend, John, 80, 90–91, 92–93
Legrand, Michel, 11–12, 13, 14–15, 41–42, 43,
    44e, 117n.7
  See also *Demoiselles de Rochefort, Les* (1967);
    Parapluies de Cherbourg, Les (1964)
Lion King, The (1994), 45–46
Lionsgate, 20, 22, 26
Lott-Lavigna, Ruby, 107
"Love in the Fall" (*Guy and Madeline on a Park
    Bench*), 15–16, 16e, 17f
Love Me Tonight (1932), 45–46
"Lovely Night, A"
  music and lyrics of, 24, 25e, 43, 44e
  overview of, 3, 4t, 37
  references in, 51–52, 53f
Luhrmann, Baz, 20–21, 68, 114
luxe pop, 13, 14–15

Macdonald, Moira, 103–4
Madison, Ira III, 89–90
McCarthy, Todd, 101
McMillin, Scott, 61–62, 64
MGM musicals, 31, 39, 56–58, 65, 89, 106
  See also Singin' in the Rain (1952)
"Mia & Sebastian's Theme," 2–3, 4t, 18–19, 37,
    58, 97–98, 98e
Moonlight (2016), 1–2, 99–100, 108–11
Moore, Mandy
  on "Another Day of Sun," 45–46, 48, 70
  background and career of, 22
  and *La La Land*'s collaborative process, 22,
    23, 24–26
  on "A Lovely Night," 52
  on "Someone in the Crowd," 49
  on "Start a Fire," 95
  See also choreography
Moulin Rouge! (2001), 66–67, 68, 114
Muir, John, 66
musical theater, 21, 32, 61–62, 66–67

Nelson, Geoff, 59–60, 106
New Wave cinema. *See* French New Wave
nostalgia
  and film technology, 67, 69, 78
  for Golden Age film musicals, 1–2, 6–7, 30–
    32, 33–35, 67
  and intertextuality, 1–2, 6–7, 33–35, 44–45,
    60
  and jazz, 79–81, 83, 97–98
  La La Land's ambivalence about, 30–31, 33–
    34, 47, 58–59, 60, 78
  and *La La Land*'s reception, 1–2, 44–45, 59–
    60, 99–100, 103–4, 106
  racialization of, 1–2, 59–60, 79–81, 97–98,
    99–100, 106
number time, 61–62

O'Connor, Donald, 89
  See also Singin' in the Rain (1952)
Oklahoma! (1943), 51–52, 56–57
Olcese, Abby, 108
On the Town (1949), 57–58
Oscars. *See* Academy Awards, 2017
#OscarsSoWhite, 109

Palmer, Jason, 14, 16, 84
Parapluies de Cherbourg, Les (1964), 11–12, 14,
    40, 41–42, 57–58, 117n.7
Pasek, Benj, and Justin Paul, 21–22, 24, 47–48
"Planetarium," 3, 5t, 71, 73f, 102, 119n.61
Platt, Marc, 23, 24–26

Pogrebin, Robin, 105–6
Porter, Ryan, 96

racial masquerading, 80, 87–89, 107
racial representation, 83–86, 89–90, 92, 95, 98,
    99, 106–7
    See also whiteness
"realist musical," 6–7, 13–14, 16, 61–64, 67,
    71–74
    See also Guy and Madeline on a Park Bench
    (2009)
reception of *La La Land*
    and the 2017 Oscars mix-up, 1–2, 108–11
    backlash, 7, 99–100, 104–8, 111–12
    and nostalgia, 1–2, 44–45, 59–60, 99–100,
        103–4, 106
    parodied on *Saturday Night Live*, 99
    praise, 1–2, 99, 101–4
    and whiteness, 1–2, 59–60, 99–100, 106–7,
        108
Reed, Rex, 105–6
reflexivity, 31–32, 39–40, 41–42, 101–2
    See also backstage musical ("show musical");
        intertextuality
RKO musicals, 51–52, 88–89
Rogers, Ginger, 30, 51–52, 53*f*, 71
Royal Wedding (1951), 65, 76
Rush, Adam, 32

Saturday Night Live, 99, 100*f*
Scorsese, Martin, 32–33
Scott, A. O., 44–45, 102–3
self-referentiality. *See* reflexivity
"selling out," 3–6, 7, 37–38, 79–80, 81–82, 90,
    92–95
Shall We Dance (1937), 30, 51–52, 88–89
"show musical." *See* backstage musical ("show
    musical")
Silman, Anna, 107
Simonec, Tim, 19–20
Sims, David, 109–10
Singin' in the Rain (1952)
    film technology in, 64–65
    as key influence on *La La Land*, 120n.29
    racial appropriation in, 89
    referenced in *La La Land*, 30, 37, 39–40, 50,
        51, 54, 56–58
Smiling Lieutenant, The (1931), 42, 120n.32
"Someone in the Crowd"
    bricolage in, 39–40
    in the film's development, 22, 27

overview of, 2–3, 4*t*
    references in, 43–44, 49–50, 50*f*
Star Is Born, A (1954), 64–65
"Start a Fire," 3–6, 5*t*, 27–28, 92–95, 94*f*
Stone, Emma
    critics on, 101–2, 105–6
    in *La La Land*'s development process, 22–24,
        27–28, 64
    performance by, 63, 64, 71–73
    See also La La Land (2016)
Stormy Weather (1943), 87, 121n.51
"Summer Montage/Madeline," 3–6, 5*t*, 85–86,
    86*e*, 86*f*
Sweet Charity (1969), 49–50, 50*f*
Swing Time (1936), 30, 51–52, 88–89

Tarantino, Quentin, 32–33
Tate, Greg, 96–97
Teller, Miles, 19, 22–23
Telluride Film Festival, 102
Top Hat (1935), 52, 53*f*
Toronto International Film Festival, 102
Touch of Evil (1958), 45
Truitt, Brian, 103–4
Trump, Donald, 103, 106, 109

Venice Film Festival, 101–2
Vera-Ellen, 71
Vernallis, Carol, 67–68
virtuosic camera, 27, 62, 67–68, 69–71, 74–76, 77
virtuosity, human, 64–65, 68, 69, 71–74, 77–78
Voeltz, Richard, 59

West Coast Get Down (WCGD), 96, 97
West Side Story (1961), 30, 41, 45–46, 49–50
West Side Story (2021), 114
whip pans, 15–16, 70
Whiplash (2014), 19–20, 69–70
whiteness
    addressed by critics of *La La Land*, 1–2, 59–
        60, 99–100, 106–7, 108
    in the Hollywood musical, 80, 87–89
    and jazz in *La La Land*, 7, 79–80, 83–87, 89–
        90, 97, 106–7, 122n.15
Wilkinson, Alissa, 63

Yahr, Emily, 104–5
Yuan, Jada, 102

Zacharek, Stephanie, 101
Zeitchik, Steven, 102

Made in the USA
Monee, IL
02 July 2026